REASONABLE DRAGONS

REASONABLE DRAGONS

How to Activate the Field of Possibilities
Where Logical Magic Is the New Normal

ALISON J. KAY, PHD

ISBN: 978-1-945446-78-8

To the ever playful, loving, abundant support
all around me, helping me guide others
through these most intense and auspicious times,
as humanity goes through its greatest evolutionary leap ever!

Contents

Acknowledgments

I want to thank the tens of thousands of students, clients, subscribers, and Vibrational UPgrade™ Facebook community members of mine throughout the years for their Trust in me and their willingness to engage in this Awakening process, unfolding the magic inherent within each of us as we live on the cutting edge of the new consciousness and explore the limitless possibilities coming online now for humanity. It is my honor to do this together as a Guide, Teacher, and Mentor.

Thank you, Mom and Dad, for creating such a loving, safe, and nurturing environment for me so I could become the best possible version of me. Thank you, brothers, for your genuine love and appreciation of your one and only sister.

Thank you to my team, both physical and metaphysical, for all that they do to support this cherished work getting to the people who are seeking it: Sandy, Claire, Jess, Larissa, and Helen, to name the core. Much humble gratitude for your belief and passionate dedication for this work brought forth by this female spiritual teacher.

Introduction

There is a new form of the masculine consciousness coming forward now as the feminine and masculine aspects of consciousness rebalance. This is, at times, gender specific; yet in the grander scheme, it's an overall rebalancing within each of us and the collective whole of humanity. The new masculine is no longer the warrior and provider and prover of strength now that the old patriarchy is crumbling.

This old patriarchy was firmly established as the Church and Science took over certain aspects of life in the West, at the end of the Middle Ages and the dawn of the Age of Reason. Yet the rebalancing that is occurring now, and has been since 2012, is from the ushering in of our new Golden Age—the Age of Humanity's Spiritual Awakening. In this estimated twenty-year window for our collective shift, we are meant to be moving into a heart-based existence. This means we've been and are moving out of a time dominated by the ego-mind, the intellect. We are moving beyond glorifying all that it can produce, which has been much at the expense of the heart and the feminine. That's the first great leap. The second is stepping into our empowerment to both choose and co-create our lives, individually and collectively, rather than falling victim to our routine lives and choices.

Humanity's Spiritual Awakening has been going on since approximately 2012. This has brought an increasing focus on spiritual wisdom, frequently in the form of ancient wisdom. Notice the emphasis on the word *wisdom*. This doesn't mean this new era is only for the younger generations, as they do not yet have the wisdom to temper their more awakened systems that they were born with. There are many baby boomers and Generation Xers who have the wisdom within spiritual communities and even outside them, who are needed to bring in this balance with the most robustness possible.

The heart has its own field of consciousness, and it is vast. As a thirty-year student of consciousness, I have been surprised by how many hidden powers of life, beyond the common sayings and understandings, reside in the heart chakra or energy center. It is a powerhouse! In this potent field are magical capacities that are becoming re-awakened now, as we move out of the Age of Reason and into the Age of Humanity's Spiritual Awakening. This coherent field that an awakened, opened heart can form carries within it capacities and possibilities beyond what the mind can ever construe. It is beyond reason.

Taking action presently looks different; it is not dependent on a plan that the mind has figured out.

Instead, it looks more like when we feel an enthusiastic: *Yes! Do that!* or *Yes! Go there!* or *Yes! Respond to this person's email!* or *Yes! Click on this!*

The heart's Guidance—and its guidance is vast—may show up in a really mundane way: enthusiasm. But this leads to further upliftment that ultimately causes the heart to sing. I call this *inspired action.*

The mind of today's globalized world, whether in the East or West, is not able to be relied upon quite so extensively. The mind is slower due to its innate functions in that it has, in great part, been programmed as a protective mechanism. When it's presented with the new, its job is to resist and inspect for potential dangers or problems.

However, the high golden frequencies that have been pouring down onto our planet since the Galactic Opening on December 21, 2012, have sped things up, specifically because they're higher frequencies, so they're faster. The mind can't keep up. Consequently, this further defers us to the tool that has been designed to work within this kind of a higher, more spiritual field—the heart.

Check in for a moment: Time feels quite different in the past few years. Do you notice it too?

Learning to allow the heart to lead—rather than the mind, with its neat plans or its own self-determined timeline of when certain achievements should occur or how they should be accomplished—is a choice based on logic, reason, and wisdom. It's simply an elevated, more complete, informed, and updated form of reason. Additionally, the need to let the heart lead—to lean into your genuine yesses—further takes you out of the heaviness of the obligations the mind perceives and lives from.

Also, there is interference within this process. Some would say we are engaged in a *Star Wars* type of light-versus-dark gig going on right now on Planet Earth; some would even say this is galactic. I am not saying either way, but I have different observations, based on my life and the lives of thousands of people I've worked with. I daily engage in clearings, activations, teachings, and mentoring so that these folks can Align their lives with their heart's desires and purpose. I've seen the dark when they go heavy with the mind's conclusions of their obligations and reasons they can't be, do, or act on the inspired new guidance, or when they go into fear or doubt, slow down, and even stop. This further embracing of the mind's doubts and fears—darkness—actually perpetuates the dark.

Living from the heart's guidance, with spiritually inclined wisdom and innate wiring, invites increasingly more light. As folks allow their minds to dominate and slip into what can be justified as logical or rational thinking—in other words, time or energy levels, checking accounts, or current obligations—they stop the increase of light. I've seen over and over again how the mind attempts to stop the expansion into the new. The heart, *not the mind,* accesses the new.

Yet, people can loop back into seemingly logical reasoning that blocks this expansion. They must create an opening for learning to live in this new way. That's where my Vibrational UPgrade™ System of support via energy medicine, mindfulness, and increased comfort in the body comes in. This is needed because as the old—living from a mind-dominant existence—gives way to the new—living from a heart-centered existence—the mind naturally resists opening to the new. The mind wants to stop the new from being seeded and locks us into the same old choices. It's called *resistance,* and we have many examples we can readily point to, both personally and globally.

Learning to live from the heart, rather than glorify the ego-mind and the intellect, is brand new for most cultures in this globalized, post-modern world. All of what has gained glory for the masses is that university, or that company, or that brand name or that car, so they can keep up with what is somehow agreed upon as the most evident truth of who is better than whom. It has been a race fed by dominance, greed, and power-over-others, yet increasingly, it has been hidden within the valuing of the intellect.

I know; I have a PhD. For my bachelor's degree, I majored first in psychology, then mass communications via examining advertising and marketing; then on to my third major of STPEC—"Social Thought Political Economy"—and finally settled upon studying this all through an art form, my fourth major: English literature, with a concentration in creative writing.

My first career and then my master's degree were in politics, public administration, and public policy, with much concentration examining environmental conservation policy. My second career was teaching. I chose teaching once I had come to understand that change has to happen person by person and collective change had not yet hit critical mass. I incorporated my energy medicine and wellness sessions alongside classroom teaching, helping folks learn to thrive more in body, mind, and spirit.

I've taught in international schools that tracked students for the Ivy League. I have traveled and lived in major international cities and all over the world. While I was offered this same lifestyle, I authentically chose what my heart and Guidance showed me was real and true, rather than what Others' ego-minds had agreed upon as necessary to prove my worth and fit in. The ego-mind's way is based on glorification of itself and the intellect, fed to us by a patriarchy that at some point meant good—or perhaps never did. Perhaps it was always about power and control. That doesn't matter anymore.

That ego-based-living gig, characterized by power over another and striving for control over another, is up. *It's about power over ourselves now*. Going inside is first. Once we then mindfully and consciously relate with others outside ourselves, it's with cooperation and collaboration, not competition and one-up-manship. It's also why we've been seeing increasing *bromances* as this new way emerges.

We are now in the second phase of the twenty-year window of Humanity's Spiritual Awakening. Dividing this window into roughly three segments of seven years each, starting in 2012, we are past the clearing, cleansing, massive purging, and shake-up mode. Now, we are building this new Golden Age. We are building with a heart-centered approach that balances the new masculine and the new feminine. They are more in harmony now, including with the Earth.

I've lived and traveled throughout our world. I've seen the heart's qualities valued in other cultures, where smiles and acknowledgment of a person's true essence are part of that first greeting: *Namaste* in India or *Sawadee Ka* in Thailand.

Compare that with the typical conversation in U.S. culture, in which people often first ask: *What do you do?* as if asking for one to prove their worth through their work—or not. Focusing on the doing feeds the asker's ego-mind so it can label and judge the other, based on their assessment of the other's response.

Equality based on our collective humanity is, in great part, what is being reset now. As we move out of the Age of Reason and into heart-based living in the northern and western societies, this will likely have echoes at an unconscious level of familiarity, from long ago. Yet we've not recently lived in a heart-led society, in which the heart guides organization, structure, and values of society.

Rather, it has been done by the mind, reason, and linearity based mostly on Newtonian physics. Within the heart, there's the power of the spirit, the soul, and a connection to the eternal. Both the Taoist and Yogic sages believe that the Spirit resides in the heart chakra. In these new times, we're building based on purpose and passion from a deeper, more eternal space.

The ego-mind may seem wild, with its erratic fears, doubts, worries, and lack of focus and concentration. By moving into a more disciplined mind, we access the heart because we've created room for it, due, in part, to valuing it. Making room for the eternal, the soulfulness, the meaning of life, also makes room for an authentic wildness, a *rewilding* for many.

Wildness comes from being alive, connected to the Vital Life Force, and living from its aliveness coursing throughout the mind-body-spirit trinity that we each are. This Vital Life Force Energy—*chi, ki, qi,* or *prana*—inherently contains an unpredictability and resembles quantum physics more than Newtonian physics. Sudden quantum leaps and other behaviors typical within the quantum world are also accessed from being this awakened and alive. This is living spontaneously. It is a large portion of the rebalancing of the masculine with the feminine.

As we follow the mind, we follow the old. As we allow ourselves to tune in to our bodies and hearts, we can *feel*. We are becoming more embodied and in touch with how our bodies respond to various stimuli, such as foods, people, places, music, movements, and events, rather than living solely in our heads. This is indigenous to the second phase of our Awakening.

As our transpersonal, more transcendental chakras above our heads become activated—and we move from the old third-dimension, seven-chakra system into a fifth-dimension, twelve-chakra system—we are given more impetus to connect with the eternal parts of existence, all the way up to more cosmic and galactic awareness. It's another indication that our consciousness is becoming even more awakened to the macrocosm. We're building now from this awareness. It is not coincidence that there has been renewed interest in space exploration and the ensuing discovery of both new planets and hospitable zones in which new planets may later be discovered. As we explore the outer reaches of galaxies not heretofore able to have been explored via modern day space exploration, much more is opening.

What is being awakened now gives us an indication of where we're headed. As with energy, sensing what is being awakened is subtle. It requires one to be able to slow down and activate the *inner detective* enough to see the clues pointed out via our Guidance from the Universe. Then, our charge is to live in accordance with them. This is the purest definition of what *yoga* means. From Sanskrit to English, yoga translates into *to yoke with*. That means to yoke with the Divine. Increasingly. And then, to co-create with the Divine. Increasingly.

With more of our transpersonal chakras awakened, and the old 3D ones fully opened and flowing the Vital Life Force Energy through them, we also have become more alive. That is part of the design now.

Living from the mind dulls down the Life Force and our aliveness; it deadens existence.

Living from the heart and an awakened system that has the Vital Life Force Energy flowing throughout it creates a more alive, connected, and purposeful existence.

You can see from the shifts in advertising and other major shifts in our healthcare systems, employment trends, small businesses, self-startups, and the increasing modernization of the old institutional religions a desire for greater living from soulfulness and aliveness.

When you tune in to the Vital Life Force Energy, you can feel its aliveness. You can see it rippling all throughout nature: folks interacting with smiles on their faces, working together to construct something new—and I do not mean just physical structures. There is an unpredictability and aliveness to this, and that's what we need to be tuning in to now. This is what is leading us forward.

We have left behind the old paradigm about destruction; we have moved into a new paradigm of our Awakening times of construction. And this is to be heart led. It's not meant to be deadened by a plan where all has to be figured out before starting. Plans frequently stop folks in their tracks before actually implementing the new.

When we build something new based on the heart's Guidance, it's alive, spontaneous, and comes in via inspiration. Frequently, this is only one to three steps at a time, and it's organic. This is also where I come in, rather robustly, to mentor folks with my energy medicine and frequencies I access on their behalf. I help them shift out of the ego-mind's dominance and the old societal expectations of *the how*. I've got their backs with my Guidance, as I activate and clear within their consciousnesses their own capacities to tune in to their Guidance, and increasingly live from it. It's like I'm running alongside them on their bike with training wheels until they can ride on their own.

Living this way is different. It requires new tools, one of which is Trust. Trust is Surrendering into the Universe and your own Higher Self having your back. You're safe and all life is working in your favor, not against you. You are not required under threat of failure to have figured it all out before starting.

This book explores tools like Trust and much more. In fact, you've already been receiving charged transmissions within the energy behind these words that is helping you to be spatula-ed up off ye olde frying pan of yesteryear, and onto the cooler, yet hopping surface of fertile soil that's just waiting for your seeds of the new life your heart is guiding you toward. As each of us becomes freer and freer, we serve the rest of humanity following behind us. We have done it before them, so it's easier when they get there. It's all happening now for everyone, only some of us are more advanced than others.

I thank you for being that advanced person you are, which has you here, reading these words and receiving the massive clearinghouse this book is. The words in this book are infused with energy transmissions downloaded to you in order to activate latent keys, codes, and your own Knowing to bring forth your greatest potential now. This then also affects the whole exponentially, with *our* greatest potential becoming increasingly activated, collectively, and lived from. There is much magic infused within the pages of this book. I do this to help move humanity forward with more grace and ease—and out of gratitude to you for being *who you be*—so you can have more fun being alive in that-there lovely body of yours on Planet Earth right now. This is how we create a future that excites you and me and is one worthy of our beloved humanity and Earth.

Yes?

CHAPTER ONE

From Nattering to Paradise

THE MIND MISLABELS, MISJUDGES, AND MISEVALUATES EVENTS

Living from the mind *limits life*. It mainly reduces the whole of life into parts with its labels, judgments, and evaluations. We can't count on the mind when we want to create something new because these labels are frequently based on misinformation due to wounding, traumas, conditioning, and other sources we'll explore. These misperceptions lead to the majority of suffering, as the Buddhist scriptures teach. The suffering—carried by the people who come to me for help—confirms this.

The Buddhist canon has, at most, fifty labels for different states of mind. These fundamental states of mind are called *factors*. Some are considered wholesome, others unwholesome. The bulk of the Buddhist teachings and meditation practices present how to use the tools of cultivating more wholesome factors, while reducing the unwholesome ones. The core concept is that the unwholesome states of mind, which everyone has different and varying tendencies toward, mislabel events and stimuli.

Additionally, the most recent studies in neurology and neurobiology have confirmed the ancient Buddhist and Yogic understanding—that the mind and brain are responsive, alive, and can change and grow depending on what we do with them.[1]

Damage to the brain or mind is no longer considered permanent. The mind is completely plastic, as is the brain; they are able to change and grow. This quality is called *neuroplasticity*. Once you reach adulthood, your brain is not a static lump of grey matter. The brain is meant to be worked with. A lot of people in the midst of suffering feel that their unwholesome and uncomfortable state of mind will never change. But this is simply not true.

The availability of constant change is simply not represented throughout our orthodox, Western, scientific, medical, nor educational training, unless it considers the most recent discoveries in quantum physics. Our typical Western training conditions us unconsciously to conceive of reality in certain ways. But when we work within a society that

---

1 Buddha pulled five of the eight main branches of Yoga – the *Eight Limbs* – out of the Yogic Path to then teach solely about the mind, with Buddhism and its focus on working only with the mind and meditation practices.

values energy and the wholeness of the mind-body-spirit trinity, the nature of life includes flexibility and dynamic change that are propelled by the innate pull of growth and expansion.

The Western psychiatric canon is problem focused.

Do you have any idea how fully this focus conditions your beliefs as to what is actually possible in life?

What about possibilities, what about living in new circumstances and new opportunities that can blast into your life and take you beyond what you have known before?

The answer to that question represents the whole other end of the spectrum; instead of problem-centric and closed-off due to suffering, this end of the spectrum is perpetual renewal. All the unlimited possibilities flow from here.

The Ego-Mind's Inherent Design Limits Its Capacity

I started my bachelor's program with a major in psychology. After three semesters, it was clear that the field of study would explore only the hardwiring of the brain and its application to things like industrial management and human resources. There had been no explanation, nor presentation, of information that told us how to be the happiest, most joyous, healthiest, thriving versions of ourselves.

One of the most helpful aspects that I have since learned as I've been studying and teaching meditation, Buddhism, yoga, qi gong, and ancient secrets from my life and studies in the East, is that the ego-mind has been given to us to help us carve out a linear framework in what is actually a nonlinear existence. Despite the mainstream scientific paradigm as presented in the West, we exist in a multidimensional world.

The mind is only one part of our mind-body-spirit trinity. Our holistic system supports us while here on Planet Earth. Our consciousness is localized in a human body while living within a multidimensional reality.

We're given this ego-mind to navigate the physical plane and to make sense of all the data that come at our five senses. When teaching AP Psych in the classroom, I was reminded that there are two separate chapters in any western Psych 101 textbook for sensing, then perceiving, data. Our five senses first pick up, or *sense,* a cue in the environment. In come those data, which are then *perceived*—the second part of the process.

This perceptual part of the process involves the classification of anything and everything our senses pick up from the outside world. In order to do this, our mind automatically goes through its pre-existing files to find out how to label this sensory-data. This labeling can only be done by *what already exists in the files.*

Meaning, the labels we use for this new thing we perceive in the environment via our five senses is always based on what it has—and *only* what it has—previously experienced. A data file to tell us what a sensory stimulus is only exists from something we've experienced sensorily before. So, when we come across something new, our mind does not yet have a data file on it.

Furthermore, the ego-mind picks up data from the external environment and classifies these external stimuli as dangerous or safe. This is because the mind is geared to protect us from danger and thus also involves the fight-or-flight mechanism. It is wired in one of our oldest regions of the brain, referred to as the *reptilian brain*. It helps us navigate the metaphysical plane we are actually in, making sense out of all the data coming at our five senses, as well as keeping us safe. Yet this has its limits, and some—including me—say this is an outdated function, considering that the majority of us no longer live in jungles facing "lions and tigers and bears—oh my!"

For example, let's say we're in Asia at a fruit stand, and we grew up in Europe. We see a piece of fruit that we do not recognize; nonetheless, our mind, based on the data, logic, and reason that we're at a fruit stand, labels the item: *fruit*. But then it searches through its files for what kind of fruit. It does not have that file because the fruit is exotic; this fruit is new to the mind. So, as a secondary step, the ego-mind then looks for what it knows is similar to this exotic fruit—*oh! A pear!*—so it labels the fruit: *Asian pear*.

As you can see, this is limiting and living based on the past. And when we're going to enter into an entirely new environment, or up-level our lives into a new, expanded arena, these inherent ego-mind mechanisms cause our ego-mind to make us have thoughts that naturally pull us back from the new. Extrapolated to a bigger usage, applied to a larger context, the basic functions are just that: basic.

Also contributing to fooling us to into believing in the conditioning we live in a linear, 3-D existence is that our five physical senses have certain thresholds put on them. This is because in a metaphysical, multidimensional reality, in a physical body on the physical Earth, there is so much data that if our physical five senses could perceive it all—if our minds were that busy—we'd go nuts.

The Creator of this brilliant human system of ours saw fit to place thresholds on how much data our physical five senses can pick up. The interesting thing here is that once we establish a steady meditation practice, and our consciousness begins to expand, these thresholds lessen. We're able to access more data from the multidimensional or metaphysical realms.

The Universe And The Soul Communicate In Symbolism

Connecting with the Metaphysical doesn't rely on logic and reason. Nor does it rely on literal translations when attempting to interpret symbols and signs as to the possible meanings behind why they appear in our lives when they do.

When all time and space seem to collapse, you're just there in the moment:

- In awe of and befuddled by the significance of that feather on the ground right in front of you
- Receiving the exact information appearing in front of your eyes when you'd been asking about it
- This person saying that very thing to you at that very moment
- That bird showing up right in front of you when going to meet a special new someone

When there's this stillness surrounding your viewing of the event, that's *synchronicity,* and it carries a symbolic message.

It's that stillness—plus that extra special feeling or tone, that accompanies the event, physical object, or person showing up saying what they do when they do—that surrounds this occurrence and communicates the message: *Pay attention to this!*

Synchronicity occurs from beyond your everyday rational, linear, logical mind. It comes in from an expanded, yet embodied, consciousness that has opened up the right brain, where the spiritual consciousness resides. Your Higher Self is accessed here, too, as well as via the heart chakra, which helps the accurate interpretation of the event's significance symbolically.

There are different Universal laws that govern the metaphysical world more than the physical. Look at that prefix, *meta*. It means *beyond*. *Meta*-physical means *beyond the physical*. If we want to interact with and understand life around us beyond the physical, then that means we have to explore beyond the mind, beyond those sensory perceptual thresholds that I just spoke of, and beyond the literal.

To do that, we have to understand the language used by the Universe, the soul, and the eternal parts of existence that are always alive. The Universe and our souls use the language of symbolism.

For example, what symbolism is at work in the weird dreams we have?

Symbolism is not literal. This is where I see a lot of people create unnecessary suffering. The ego-mind—and even more specifically, logic and reason within the functioning of the left brain—is limited to literal interpretations. I witnessed some of my more literal students in English Literature struggle with this new symbolic language while studying units on symbolism within Oscar Wilde's and Edgar Allen Poe's works. The left brain and the ego-mind function based on cognitive data. Thus, they misinterpret what the soul and the Universe desire us to know, or they entirely miss the messaging.

My mentoring frequently involves teaching the new language of symbolism. The Universe is always there. The greater, nonlocalized field of consciousness, of *Universal Life Force,* or *chi* (aka *qi, ki*), or *prana,* is alive and constantly speaking to us, especially when we are awake and interactive with it. We can ask it to show us signs or give us messages.

To interpret this different language of symbolism requires that we move beyond the ego-mind's preference for familiarity, logic, and reason to access things like synchronicities. Events come together, with the timing of the information ultimately landing in your life as perfectly, communicating exactly what you need, whether this is simply supportive inspiration in which you feel without a doubt that all will be well, or it actually is a person providing a service you've been looking for but unable to find. To experience more synchronicities, and increasingly live your life from here—where everything seems to magically come together—necessitates learning how to move beyond simply living from the ego-mind and the left brain's logic and reason.

Preferring Reason When You Are In Intuition's Domain Leads To Suffering

One of my all-time favorite quotes is often attributed to Einstein: *A human being's most important choice is whether they view the universe as friendly or hostile.*

It is so illustrative of his understanding that life operates at a subatomic level. That's at a subconscious, or unconscious level, meaning this occurs *below the radar of the conscious mind.* Therefore, what occurs in energy and consciousness (subtle energies) precedes and is more influential than what occurs in physical matter. Our point of view creates reality, rather than our reality creating our point of view.

The hidden conclusions—meaning they fall below the radar of the conscious mind—we've collected throughout our lives come from conditioning and other sources. For example, we can have what is called an *imprint.* From ages zero to two, we do not separate our thoughts and feelings from our parents. We think what they think, we feel what they feel, without separating from them as an individual. At age two, the *terrible twos* begin, when you hear kids say no! This is because they are separating from their parents and developing individuality. This is the real beginning of the momentum for the ego-mind as a person develops their own identity. From ages two to eight, we form subconscious conclusions as we learn how the world around us works.

If, for example, we see that our older sister receives a lot of attention from our mom by being a really good student, we might conclude: *I need to be a really good student in order to get that good attention—that feeling—I want from my mom.*

That conclusion is then wired in at the subconscious level. Over and over, I've seen subconscious beliefs like this create blocks for clients.

The child-like logic in that subconscious conclusion is an element of perfectionism, which forms in a personality during ego development. Suppose a person experienced trauma because of seeking attention from a mother who left, or who experienced an over-emphasis on various factors later on, such as school or peers. The conclusion could cause that person to cling to being perfect as a part of their way of receiving approval. The block becomes more than a subconscious conclusion. It becomes more solidly hard-wired and develops as a more layered block. I've seen this frequently while helping folks unravel their most stubborn stopping or sticking points.

That is a quick example. At unconscious levels—*un* meaning *not*-conscious—or subconscious levels—*sub*-meaning *under*-conscious—conditioning is quite elusive and typically overlooked because everyone around you—the media, marketing, science, education, and the politics of your societal system—organize around this collective conditioning.

If I grew up in a society that is reliant on logic and reason to the exclusion of the benefit of listening to the intuition, then I likely have an unconscious preference for logic and reason. Additionally, I may possess an accompanying unconscious disregard for intuition. If I live in the East for ten years, let's say, and I am immersed in a culture that honors the intuition, and I have cultivated my awareness, then I may be able to recognize that distinction: *Oh, this is what it looks like when the intuitive mind is also valued!*

If I never leave my home country—or I leave my home country but don't immerse myself in another culture long enough, or I don't bother to observe the other cultures' practices, or I've not cultivated my awareness—then I might never understand that I am living with this unconscious preference. I would probably label the preferences simply *cultural differences.* I would live in a more limited way because I'd have an unconscious preference that was built upon an unconscious conclusion that came to me via my cultural—and likely, parental—conditioning. I would not know what is available beyond what parameters had been set because of the unconscious preference that guides what I look to and look for. And if I'm surrounded by folks who are all doing the same, the experience would be reinforced.

In addition to the unconscious conditioning from our parents, we receive subtle energetic conditioning from our ancestry.

Another aspect of unconscious and subconscious blocks that leads to mislabeling, mis-evaluating, and misjudging is trauma. Trauma can be from this lifetime or other lifetimes. Traumas typically reside in the subconscious. When traumas are carried over from previous lifetimes, my strenuous research and experience has led me to see it is contained in our cellular memory, within each of our DNA strands, and correlated to the relevant chakra.

Blocks, whether unconscious or subconscious, lock energy and prevent energy from flowing throughout the area of the chakra the block corresponds to. The block affects the relevant, corresponding area of the body as well. Then, the overall flow of energy throughout the mind-body-spirit trinity system is blocked in that area.

Subconsciously held traumas lead to an even more tightly automated response and have a looping sensation to them. This is an example of the mind-body connection: how the mind and body communicate, and how the mind-body-spirit system goes into a holding pattern, locked down in one feedback loop, without conscious choice or conscious control available.

We can't trust our mind's labels, judgments, and evaluations, especially when we've done little to no work with our mind and consciousness. They're simply not yielding accurate perceptions when colored with these distortions.

STOP THIS NATTERING ALREADY!

During a family outing, my dad pulled out of a parking space to make it easier for me to enter the car. While I waited, I noticed one driver in the lot allowed him the time he needed. Another driver got impatient after a few seconds of waiting and peeled out, maneuvering around my father's car as he was in the process of backing out.

Once I got in the car, some of my family reacted with "Ah, I cannot believe how impatient that person was!"

I responded to them, *redirecting* them, "But the first person was totally patient."

As seen in this example, it's so easy to flip the lever of interpretation that labels an event as *negative*. There seems to be so much accessibility to the negative. Understanding the greater context, however, can lead to increased peace.

Seeing from a greater perspective is quintessential to life right now, especially if you'd like to decrease your suffering. A mountaintop perspective—a wider understanding—is needed to comprehend what is actually being asked of us during this particular stage of humanity's evolution.

Those who are still living from the mind experience life as tight and contracted. They exhibit less patience. Without a broader awareness or the tools to aid themselves, they thus live in a more generalized resistance at their core. They are missing the massive shift many of us are currently undergoing. Nonetheless, they receive the higher frequencies of our Awakening times.

Even if you have no practices whatsoever, or if you consider yourself agnostic or atheist, you're still receiving these higher frequencies, which are meant to benefit you. You're still being influenced by the energetics that continue to pour down upon us so that humanity shifts. How you respond or react to these new, different, and intensified events in the outside world, along with the new subtle influences you're experiencing within your inner world—what you label, judge, or evaluate them as—absolutely dictates how much suffering you experience in this moment.

The incessant mislabeling of things and events as *bad* and *negative* perpetuates a hungry, Pacman-esque energy for more of the same. The whining and nattering *in which the mind naturally engages* fuels this negativity. This is the Buddhist's acknowledgment of the mind when in its unwholesome state. My very first signature talk, which I've been giving and teaching in my weekly yoga and meditation classes for twenty-five years, is "The Nature of the Mind." In this fundamental teaching, I speak to the ego-mind's inherent tendency in these post-modern, globalized times to focus on the negative—to churn out the negative—complaining thoughts. By focusing on the negative, you feed it and it grows. This reflexive reaction is in exact opposition to the higher vibrations that shift us out of the mind and into the heart, where we are meant to feel more at ease, relaxed, and with a sense of well-being, as our inherent birthright.

The Increase In Suffering: Do You Feel It?

You can see suffering in so many different places right now, such as in shopping malls, markets, traffic, news, world politics, and online. Fear and ensuing resistance are happening at an unconscious level, in reflexive resistance to this massive change being commanded across our planet.

Yet there are also those who have become even more patient, compassionate, and understanding; likely, you are one of them. You have been following your Guidance even when it doesn't make sense. You are reading this book, seeking answers, and following your heart's desire to open your life more. This opening is the core of what is being energetically fed to us now as an undercurrent.

The opposite of opening is to close down further. We can see more violence and divisiveness in the form of human activity, such as mass shootings; as well as in natural occurrences, such as volcanic eruptions, floods, hurricanes, and fires. All this has led to an increased potential for contracting and tightness as a possible state of mind in reaction to these higher vibrations if we're not conscious and aware of it. Leaving the discussion of global warming and its impacts aside for now, and resuming that mountaintop perspective, you can see that these higher vibrations are here to catalyze us to learn to live in a different, more heart-centered way. Right?

That's what I frequently see when folks begin to work with me. It is especially true among those who have done less work on their own minds. I've seen this both in myself since my first days as a meditator, as well as in others while teaching meditation. The ego-mind's reaction to more lightness and upliftment is fear.

Thus, shifts and changes—as we grow more aligned with and into who we're here to be—catalyze the ego-mind's reactive, reflexive resistance to this change. Some of it is also due to our old, reptilian brain wiring that keeps us safe.

Our growth on the spiritual path includes the eternal experience of being a soul in a body here to experience life and grow, or to remain within an ego-mind, personality-dominant existence, in which we perpetuate the same old behaviors, crises, and cycles, never evolving beyond them. We may remain stuck in an existence based on the ego-mind identity, personality and materialistic level, never opening to living from a more expanded consciousness, beyond just that part of us. It's easy to get stuck at that physical level, or at least it used to be. That option has been so loud and so reinforced, societally.

The essence of this change now is a rebalancing of the spiritual and the material in all ways, with all the connotations and far-reaching impacts from within each of us out and up through our organization of societies and institutions. The connotations and impacts also flow back down to how we treat each other, our bodies, our aliveness, our spirituality, our money, our Earth. There has been, and continues to be, such a massive influx of frequencies. They are meant to elevate our thoughts and further harmonize us with how we view our existence and what we're here to be and do.

What If It's Not What Your Mind Says It Is?

An actress in my Magic, Manifestation, and Money Flow program recently shared on a call last week one of the key areas of suffering for her that she's increasingly letting go of during the course of the program.

Her mind has been demanding:

When are you going to land that specific role?

When are you going to experience that critical breakthrough?

Why has it not happened yet?

Her ego-mind has been directing her to focus on the *when* and the *how*—and doing so in a mean way.

What if:

- The issue is not what her mind says it is?
- There's nothing wrong?

- *Not getting that role* is actually testing her to see what she's willing to open up to?

And what if her not simply going with the familiar, and instead saying no to the same old kind of role, further opens her up, strengthening her command: *I will have more than that, yes please!* to a new possibility coming in?

In this case, what I perceive will happen is based on how I've seen the Universe work countless times: It readjusts itself based on the energy of a person's new vibration. It needs this new input when the person is in an expansion stage so it can clarify what they now desire and match it. And it needs time to do this.

For the actress in the class, the Universe will eventually deliver a brand-new opportunity that will be a better match for her desires and is meant to go with her career, and the results will be more fulfilling for her. It is no irony that this new direction will bring forth her most innate gifts and talents. This happens all the time with my clients and students.

Again, interpreting events literally and from the ego-mind causes the chopping off of one's self at the knees. Rather, when seeing symbolically and living from more of that mountaintop perspective, this Aligns your desires with the new energy. Thus, from this increased detachment and mountaintop perspective, you're living more from the heart chakra's aspects, like *Allowing* and *Receptivity,* which yield different interpretations of what's happening in the world and in your life, instead of what the nattering mind clamors on and on about regarding what's wrong.

Not only do accurate interpretations get allowed of what your Soul and the Universe is up to that are gentler and more expansive for you, but you're also actually increasing the emanation and magnetism of your desires by shifting in this way. This then activates more of consciousness to do the heavy lifting for you.

I know you have heard this by now: *living from the heart*.

But what if even that is not what you think it is?

There's a systematic science to the way consciousness behaves, and that especially comes into play with the potent capacities of the heart chakra. There are certain tools and processes that you can learn that will help you live from a gentler, more expansive space and from there you can invite in more Life Force, too, to benefit you in your life.

Moving Beyond The Pre-Requisites (2012–2032)

When I moved back to the States after my decade in Asia, within the first two years I was approached by Voice America Talk Radio Network to host a show on the Mayan, or the Galactic, Alignment of December 21, 2012. At the time, my work was not at all focusing on that. I was continuing to look at the science behind consciousness, coupled with the ancient practices of working with consciousness for improved well-being, vitality, and fulfillment. So, this was a bit *out there* for me.

I mis-labeled this possibility because I had my own preferences still shaped and imprinted by my home society's preference for being grounded in logic, reason, and science. I ended up tracing through the development of that societal preference for logic and reason and its distaste for the intuitive, intangible, and holistic, in my first book, written during my last year in Asia, *What If There Is Nothing Wrong?*

Nonetheless, I considered the possibility of having my own radio show on the Galactic alignment of December 21, 2012. My internal GPS—my whole body—aligned with a big, neon, billboard-sized YES.

So, I did it. I began the initial shows by interviewing scientists who have developed cutting-edge tools and techniques for measuring consciousness and sharing what scientists have validated about the chakra system and other ancient secrets. I interviewed thought leaders and scientists and folks connected to the Dalai Lama who I'd worked with for my first book. Some of these are the pioneers who'd conducted the first scientific measurements of the effects of meditation. I interviewed specialists about the Galactic alignment of December 21, 2012, and the world really began to open in an entirely new way that I had not expected.

I came to understand the nature of these times we're in: We are now in a twenty-year window, from 2012 to 2032, of Humanity's Spiritual Awakening, and this is considered our greatest evolutionary leap ever! My second book, *Vibrational UPgrade™—A Conspiracy for Your Bliss: Easing Humanity's Evolutionary Transition,* delves extensively into the meaning of our Spiritual Awakening, and why it's considered our greatest evolutionary leap ever. In fact, much of what I learned from interviewing these scientists and experts is provided in that book.

One of the reasons it's considered to be our greatest evolutionary leap ever is that within the next twenty years, we are going to be moving through two levels of entirely different paradigms and living. In fact, this is considered an even bigger leap in evolution than when we humans began walking upright.

At the same time I was interviewing scientists and specialists, I was asked to be a yoga teacher, speaker, and energy medicine specialist on a December 2012 cruise to the Mayan ruins in the Yucatan with these other specialists. We traveled to the Mayan ruins, and we'd received special permission to work with a Mayan shaman on the day of the Galactic alignment.

The ground was buzzing! There were film crews there from around the world; apparently, I was seen on TV that reached as far as Poland. I had been to Chichen Itza just the year before, taking a VIP client on a retreat to the sacred sites. Yet the ground was not buzzing through my bare feet then the way it was at this point on December 21, 2012.

After I returned from this extraordinary trip, I kept doing my radio show and interviewing more specialists. I ended up talking about things like crop circles and other phenomena that point to this being a really auspicious time, both in the Universe and on Planet Earth.

As another influence of these Awakening times we're in, I've observed myself, gradually and increasingly, within my own yoga practices, my yoga and meditation regular classes I teach, in interviews, and within my talks given to my students, clients and subscribers, have an increased focus on the alignments that were happening in the stars.

It seems abundantly clear that there are major historical events that have changed humanity forever with the same astrological alignments consistently since 2012. I found that on NASA.com, you can see alignment after alignment in the stars, hinting at the same specialness of this time. They refer to astronomical events that haven't happened for five hundred years, or since the time of Christ's birth or other major world events, such as the Berlin Wall coming down.

There is something going on. I can smell it and logically piece it all together. I've learned to pay attention to the subtle guidance of the Universe—the events it Guides me to see as I've increasingly cultivated my higher consciousness and tuned in. Yet I've done this while remaining steeped in logic and reason and at a macrocosmic, societal, and global level, not just focused on individuals.

The combination of managing both the mountaintop perspective to piece together the clues that my higher consciousness picks up on and remaining firmly grounded in my body down on Planet Earth allows me to absorb this information with an elevated application of logic and reason. I have learned to pay absolute attention to the Universe's clues via my GPS. And I give to you the benefits of this, to make it easier for us all, so the most robust possibilities ensue for us as we move into this new Golden Age.

The ancients from all corners of the Earth looked to the stars. That was their nightly entertainment. It continues as part of the science of advanced yoga practices, of opening up to all that exists, so we can connect our consciousness and body with this inspiration via the stars and their alignments. We do this through our chakra column—through our consciousness flowing throughout our mind-body-spirit system via our chakras—the more we clear our blocks and purify our ego-mind.

There is something magical going on right now and very much of it is about shifting out of living from a mind dominant system and into living from the heart and all the magic that ensues from there. There are actual techniques for doing so that I consistently present to the folks who work with me. Shifting from a mind-dominant to heart-centered way of living is the first level.

The second level involves learning to use your lower human will and subverting that to your higher consciousness's will so you are co-creating with Divine, or as in yoga, *yoking with the Divine.*

A huge amount of power is being given to us. Everybody is at a different level of accessing it and being allowed to access it.

YOUR MIND HAS A DOOR THAT OPENS THE GATEWAY

I see people drawn to working with the Laws of Attraction. When they are ego-mind dominant, they work with the laws for a little bit of time and then evaluate: *This does not work.*

It's true that it does not work, not if you try it once or twenty times, if you are trying it only from your mind. The mind will come in with the *this does not work judgment* as a natural part of learning to move beyond living from the mind.

The mind also comes in with a series of labels:

- *It has not worked yet.*
- *Why has this not worked yet?*
- *This must not work.*

Yet this seems to be part of the purification, or initiation, process to move beyond the mind's desire to stop you from opening to more. Some traditions refer to this process as *The Lifting of the Veil.*

What we are talking about here is the enlightenment process within the yogic path. By this, I mean the cleaning of the dominance of the ego-mind—including where it has become distorted from the impacts of our conditioning, unconscious preferences and subconscious traumas, and subconscious and unconscious imprints. These are all gradually addressed and cleared when *remaining consistently at the process of The Lifting of the Veil.* It is a process—a path. I've done everything I can to speed this up, and I do facilitate really quick shifts in folks, quicker than how long it took me! Nonetheless, *the practice does require consistent focus.*

When you live from the mind, the mind hides that there is even a veil to lift, because it's still operating from behind the veil, with these very conclusions:

- *This hasn't worked yet; it must not work.*
- *None of this metaphysical spiritual stuff works.*
- *It is just woo-woo; let me go back to the understanding that only what can be seen is what can be believed.*

Your mind has mislabeled the process and life itself because you've not yet cleared enough distorted perceptions to move beyond the mind. The process of clearing seems a bit circular on purpose, to keep it hidden from those not ready.

If you are going to access the power to co-create and wield energy so you can ultimately relatively affect matter, of course a purification of the ego-mind and motives has to occur. No one is going to be given this power when they may be destructive with it.

By clearing much of this *mind-stuff* out, it seems like this is the gateway into having more access to the Universal Life Force. You know at your core that life contains lots of mysteries, many layers, and much magic to it.

You can acknowledge this much, right?

And this is the veil, and why it's referred to a process of *lifting*, or *seeing beyond*, the veil.

The Science Behind The Gateway

I present a lot of this science in my first book, *What If There Is Nothing Wrong?* There is one particular aspect of brain function which seems to be like a drawbridge being lowered, or an activation of sorts of a new level being reached. Part of the brain that is in between the right brain and left brain is called the *anterior cingulate*. When you have sustained twenty minutes of any kind of practice that takes you beyond your ego-mind—whether praying, meditating, chanting, or saying mantras—you have activated your anterior cingulate. This is the part that acts like a drawbridge lowering.

And when the drawbridge is lowered, you access your intuitive brain and spiritual brain.

I've come to understand something from twenty-six years of meditating and twenty-five years of teaching meditation around the world to all different ages and all different cultures: After ten minutes of meditation, the mind—no matter the culture, age, or gender of the meditator—seems to start gaining hard-wired, cognitive benefits, in which you experience improved focus, concentration, and memory.

Thereafter, from minutes twelve to twenty, the meditative experience is more about peace and calm, as your physiology shifts out of the sympathetic nervous system into the parasympathetic nervous system. Part of this is due to the inner-directed focus, so that outside stimuli isn't coming at you; thus, the calming occurs. Your focus on calmed breathing also helps shift your physiology.

Yet part of this is happening because the *pre-frontal cortex*—the most advanced part of our brain—becomes more involved at this stage. There have been increasing studies done by imaging on the brain during meditation, and it seems that it has become commonly acknowledged that "Prefrontal regions mediate both the preparedness of religious experience and conscious cognitive process involved in the appreciation of religious experience."[2] And this increases the calming in our physiology. If you substitute this old-school languaging of *religion* with *spirituality*, that may help you increase your understanding of what is being said here.

Then from minutes twenty to thirty, the anterior cingulate is activated. That is when the spirituality really starts to kick in because we've activated the connection to something beyond us. If we couple quantum physics with yogic terms, our individualized, localized consciousness is now connecting with, or yoking with, a nonlocalized, Greater Consciousness.

Carl Jung, Freud's student and the single most impressive aspect for me of Freud's work, coined a phrase, "the collective unconscious." This is similar to the nonlocalized consciousness I am referring to here. Carl Jung, it seems likely, took this from his studies of the Eastern classic, the *I Ching*.

I find it intriguing that there's a method of scientific study, called *Naturalist Observation,* which has been mostly left behind in our post-modern world of laboratories and controlled studies. Naturalist Observation is considered the third methodology of gathering scientific measurements and was included as one of the three main scientific methods that were originally presented during the scientific

---

2 PubMed, Azari, et al., 2001

revolution, generally marked by Copernicus' discoveries in the 1540s. It seems like it eventually became a part of the discussion of empiricism, by folks like John Locke. Yet as far back as Aristotle, and even further back, the yogic sages employed this methodology prior to "the scientific revolution."

Natural Observation is employed when you are not in the laboratory and you are not able to control the variables being measured in the study—when you observe a subject unmanipulated in its natural behavior and habitat. For five thousand years, yogic sages had been using Naturalist Observation to study meditators and what meditation leads to. Their findings are documented in yogic sutras and Buddhist canons that address how to work with the various states of the mind to move beyond suffering.

In these Awakening Times, when we're able to access higher states of consciousness gained through meditative practices, how do we work with the Life Force that has been freed up from our blocked chakras?

Based on the empiricist evidence that these are new times with new levels of consciousness and vibrations able to be reached, they require some new questions, new processes, and new tools.

How do we work with this consciousness to cultivate even more than we are taught in yoga or qi gong or Reiki?

It seems that there is a great potential ripening and waiting for us to open as if unwrapping a present on our birthday. And I get to live my day-to-day life discovering this new potential as I work with and on behalf of the potential of my clients, students, and the greater collective, because what each of us achieves has a holographic effect. Thus, I continue to work within the *hundredth monkey* theory. This has become my political action nowadays. As each person uplifts, they then uplift the whole. And in these new times, with the higher vibratory backdrop, the effects are that much more exponentialized.

Why You Want To Go To This Land

When you allow your mind to simply roam wherever it wants and glorify your intellect for all that it can compute, you are living at a primitive level. You are a mind, a body, and a spirit. You leave so much latent potential untapped by focusing only on the mind! Or you leave so much potential on the table, so to speak. Especially now, in these times. I hope by now you are starting to see how this perpetuates struggle, staleness, stagnancy, and dryness, when other choices are increasingly available.

When you exist merely within ego-mind dominance, you live with your mind locked into interpretations you have inherited, and you robotically repeat history. When you live from a mind-dominance that is not purified in any way, then all the aggression, impatience, and divisiveness dominate. Living from the mind promotes the mistaken idea that the ego-mind is considered the personality, or the core, of who someone really is.

And then our unconscious conclusions govern our beliefs about who somebody with the ego-mind label is or is not, and whether we prefer them, and whether we reject them as a result. All this is moving in a completely reactive, robotic, deadening, destructive, unconscious way. It is neither constructive nor creative.

Furthermore, there is a whole other level, discussed in the last chapter of my previous book. Yogic sages call this land *turiya*. This translates to a "sense of bliss with and from an ecstatic opening." You can access this bliss-giving Life Force in a way that helps you with your creations. In turiya, you do not have to push, make happen, figure out the how, or feel as if you are pushing a boulder up a mountain when you want to create a new project, venture, relationship, or life. It assists you in creating new routines and habits. The behavior of change's behavior has changed.

Support is all around you, all the time. It wants to support you, yet you have to invite it in. And the only way you invite it in is not through the way you might think, by praying or pleading for the suffering to stop. Instead, it is through more heart-based aspects like Trust and yielding. We'll talk about that more later.

But there is so much more ease and even brilliance that is available to help us with our lives right now. And to live at that most basic reactive level just seems unreasonable and illogical at this point.

The Adventure That Awaits You

My whole life, I've followed the clues and signs I've learned to interpret.

If you've been following me for a while, you've likely heard me say, "I feel like Hansel and Gretel following the bread crumbs."

I have lived in many different countries. I have lived an *extraordinary* life. I've heard my Guidance, and I know not to choose against it because the few times I have, struggling, suffering, pain, and boredom ensue. It's a charmed essence that knows and wants what's in my highest and best interest. It also knows better and can see more than I do from its nonlocalized, grand perspective.

One of my closest lifelong friends said to me, "You just do not let yourself get comfortable."

I do not. It's not because I get bored as much as it is because *I have to* listen to my Guidance, no matter what inconvenience may result initially from doing so. My Guidance shows me one plus one is two, but it is a different logic, a logic beyond that which we were taught in school. It is a bigger, more yielding kind of logic. But it pieces life together in such a brilliant way—a way in which there are open doors instead of resistance, struggle, and brick walls.

This reminds me of the traffic patterns that were seemingly absent when I first began driving—really, walking!—in Asia. Yet over time, as I began to ride a bicycle, and then quickly upgraded to a scooter for my own survival, I saw that what seemed to my Western eyes as chaos actually had a higher order to it. It was its own harmony, just one not familiar to my mind to label as harmony.

Your mission, should you choose to accept it, is simply to walk through the creation of something, rather than efforting and pushing and making it happen, ending in an exhausted heap in the corner, or pounding down lattes. Instead, when we open up to this Greater flow of Life Force Energy, there is an awakeness and aliveness that constantly feeds us.

I work with certain mechanisms in the consciousness of a person's mind, body, and spirit. The work opens their systems so they can flow and move gradually beyond unconscious and subconscious preferences, conclusions, and stuck points. Some people refer to those as *blocks*. Yet, once cleared, you can dance with the Universe and help it create through you. Here, too, there are process and key activations and clearings I do to help people open and access even more of this Vital Life Force to fuel them, their lives, and creations. I actually call myself a *chess piece for the*

Divine. Living this way is a whole lot more fun than your myopic, localized consciousness could've possibly come up with.

I cannot imagine living any other way. Think of it as the drawbridge that invites you into a magical land where you are the king or queen of your castle. I don't think it's any mere coincidence that people are looking more to unicorns, castles, dragons, Merlin, King Arthur, Queen Guinevere, and Camelot. All that legend and lore and interest in magic, including the Harry Potter phenomena in the 2000s and the *Train Your Dragon* phenomena of the 2010s, is more prevalent because we are searching for something more, something beyond our dry logic and reason.

We have a yearning for magic in our lives. Perhaps since The Age of Reason made us all into rationalists, we now yearn for something that isn't quite like that—something to counterbalance it. Perhaps the interest in magic is increasing because we are being asked to drink once more of this wisdom, as if from a mountain's ancient bubbling healing spring. The wisdom is popping open again in Humanity's Awakening Times right now.

CHAPTER TWO

Holistic Is Giving Birth to Unity

JUDGING, EVALUATING, AND LABELING SEPARATE, REJECT, AND DIVIDE

The Buddhist canon helps us understand basic functions of the mind that are so unconscious and so basic that they barely get looked at until you choose to start looking within.

I remember the first time I saw the bumper sticker:

DON'T BELIEVE YOUR THOUGHTS.

I was an undergrad and was really surprised by it because I had grown up in a household gearing me to value the intellect, logic, and what my thoughts produced, including regular *Star Trek* viewing.

In fact, questioning my thoughts was quite a radical idea for me. I had to fight my parents' desires to attend a university of my choice. I had followed the inner Guidance that helped me open up to this new world. One of the first books I read about mindfulness came from my alma mater, UMass Amherst. So, it seems this is in great part why I had fought to attend this University that I felt was such a great fit for me—because I was going to be influenced by the American mindfulness movement that was originating in the Berkshires there at the time. When I moved out West to San Francisco for my masters, I saw the bumper sticker:

QUESTION YOUR THOUGHTS.

Lessons From Elementary School

When we learn a language, we learn vocabulary. We learn to say that color is red while we also learn what the color purple looks like, and we give them both a label.

Then we unconsciously decide our preferences:

- Do we *like* red?
- Do we *like* purple?
- Which do we prefer?

Reductionism Versus Wholism

When I was writing my first book, *What If There Was Nothing Wrong?*, I found myself tracing back to the Age of Reason, when science became an institution, dividing authorities with the Church. That helped me understand how we in the West have become so reductionist and how that philosophy affects our perceptions of life.

At the time, I was living in Taiwan and embedded in a culture whose philosophy centered around *wholism.*

For a decade, I immersed myself in understanding the Chinese holistic system:

- The Chinese have an idiomatic, pictographic language that is much more holistic than written English.
- China's mode of communication is also holistic because, as a culture, it honors the group rather than the individual.
- The Chinese also tend to honor harmony, which is much more holistic than honoring the voice of an individual.
- Traditional Chinese Medicine is a holistic system that does not reduce the mind-body-spirit system into separate, individual body organs or parts without connection to each other, to the whole organism, to emotions, to state of mind, or to spirit.
- From a young age, people consume food with an understanding and appreciation of how foods interact with each other and the body because the culture supports how food is meant to be medicine.

All aspects of life are presented in this holistic paradigm.

In contrast to that here in the West, the Age of Reason separated the rational and supernatural between science and the Church. With the creation of science, authority was taken out of the hands of the alchemists, who worked from a holistic understanding of the Universe, the elements, and our place among them. Science and the Church established a formal patriarchy, and with that, a formal means of controlled study and presentation of our world. To do this, science chopped the parts from the whole, so that these discrete parts could be controlled and studied using the scientific method.

But in a reductionist paradigm such as this, the whole, formed by various parts, is lost. It's reduction, analysis, and conclusion, without consideration for the inherent role the part has both in and to the whole, which frequently changes when merging the part back into the whole. This reduction frequently leads to misconstruing the part.

It's along the same lines as our approach to nutrition. Consider that we acquire our necessary vitamins and minerals—no longer present in our soil due to industrial, mono-crop farming—from supplements taken in isolated form, like vitamin D, rather than eating whole-food forms of them, or even taking whole-food supplements. When taking a whole-food supplement, you ingest the cofactors in the whole food to help absorb and make more bioavailable the aspects of the singular vitamin or mineral you're going for. Popping a handful of singular supplements does not include the cofactors naturally occurring in the food to help you absorb that singular vitamin or mineral.

Reductionism is a misrepresentation of how things actually work, and it separates the parts for the purpose of control, power, and material gain. It does not consider the impact of the part as a piece of the whole and within the whole. When a system is treated as holistic, however, the approach involves increased appreciation for the inherent genius and magic of life. Reductionism appears, rather arrogantly, to dismiss that.

I suppose it would have made sense if, at the start of the Age of Reason, the split with the Church was so the Church could cover the whole human organism. But it was not. The body was ignored by the Church, as was the material—even with their coffers becoming the richest source for many kings, like Henry VIII. And the mind was not addressed much, save for cultivating guilt and shame, to keep folks in order.

Again, for a more thorough, in-depth exploration of this, please see my first book, *What If There's Nothing Wrong?*

Within science's domain as split during the Age of Reason, the more recent discoveries that rocked the orthodox science community were not able to be controlled and studied. As a result, they were not accepted until approximately one hundred years later. Among these are Max Planck's discovery of the matrix of interconnectivity at the subatomic level in 1918, which won him the Nobel Peace Prize.

Our science, nonetheless, has for three hundred years been based on two erroneous assumptions:

1. Everything is separate from everything else. What happens in one place has no effect on what happens anywhere else. If it looks as though it does, it's only a coincidence.

2. Our inner experience—our thoughts, beliefs, feelings, and emotions—have no effect on the world outside of and beyond our bodies. This had to be the case for a reductionist model to work.

Science, based on these two assumptions for more than three hundred years, is in no small way responsible for creating this reductionist model. This goes against what the ancient traditions in the East have known, as did our alchemists in the West: all life is interconnected, and we have the ability to influence and impact what happens outside of and around us.

We have become science-centric in the West, and science-reliant, and have the unconscious preference for things to be scientifically validated. On my radio show and for my first book, I interviewed scientists who shared with me the view that we have now leaned so far into the reductionist model that we need to come back into balance. Within some of the more cutting-edge halls of science, this has also been seen. Many of those scientists have left.

I remember when I first came back to the States from the decade in Asia, and I had my first speaking gig at a mind-body-spirit expo. I was focusing on meditation mindfulness in my first signature talk, "The Nature of The Mind." I met an integrative physician who founded a local clinic. We met afterward to see if our working together was aligned and would lead to better outcomes for everyone involved.

He looked at my resumé and unique background and said, "I would love to have you as a part of my clinic's offerings. Yet you have too much here. I don't see how it fits. You need to specialize in one thing."

This was within six months of my return from a decade of studying the value of a holistic system.

Without hesitation, I said, "No, it has to be inclusive; it's a holistic model. If we want to help people—truly help—we have to understand the mind-body-spirit trinity. That is precisely why I've achieved the specific certifications, degrees, and training to combine together as a whole so that we do not separate the individual. We treat the individual as a whole, acknowledging how their mind affects their body, how their spirit affects their body and vice-versa, and how to improve well-being."

We realized we were not a good fit. I continued to cultivate and develop my holistic work.

Do You Plan To Remain At A Basic Level?

Staying at a basic level does not seem like the Universe's plan for us right now!

When I attune and train others in energy medicine, I teach that there's an innate intelligence to Vital Life Force. No worries. The energy knows where to go and what to do—and what not to do. It's not up to them. For example, when someone comes in complaining of chronic back pain, I may be led to work with their knees or neck, not directly with their back. Always, *always, the energy knows better;* it knows what to prioritize in order for well-being and balance to be restored.

I teach how to Trust and Surrender to the wisdom beyond what our ego-mind can reason. Surrender is *the* key to accessing the higher knowing inherent in the Universal Life Force. It's there. Furthermore, this Vital Life Force is wanting to flow throughout our systems and around us at all times. It's called *Vital Life Force Energy*. Vital means alive. It is behind all life.

To stop pushing against, resisting, or being frustrated with life, as if in some perpetual battle, this increasing Surrendering to a Higher Knowing within you and the

Universe is a key. All that ego-mind stuff has a heavy or tense or forceful energy when life is done from there.

A natural elegance and grace and flow that we can live from makes everything easier when we yield to its innate intelligence. You can learn how to do that increasingly. At some stage, this will get to the point where you want to do it because you see how much smarter this Universal Life Force is than you. The electricity, magnetism, and light are so much easier to create from when you learn to work with Life Force, rather than against it. It is much more perfected and loving than your own ego-mind.

REJECTION VERSUS INCLUSION

This basic understanding of the mind I have seen radically change the levels of joy and ease in peoples' lives. The mind and its thinking of thoughts—being the thought factory that the mind has become—is the nature of the mind.

Labeling Leads To Rejection

Think about the last thing you said no to.

There is a sense of pushing it away, right?

And in that pushing away, that rejection of that thing that you said no to—or that person or that event—there is a subtle element of force or aggression.

Now, feel into the last time you said yes to something.

There is a feeling of yielding or softness or welcoming, right?

This is Surrendering.

There is an implied and subtle effect when we say *that color is red,* and *this color is purple*. We have labeled; that's first.

Then, there is an implied question of preference of one to the other.

In that separation—from a *this-or-that* way of perceiving, from wholeness down into parts, from forming words followed by the unconscious and automatic focus of *which one do I prefer?*—there is a level of rejection.

Evaluation leads to a label, which leads to the rejection that contains varying levels of force and aggression and pushing away. Coming to the preference of one and rejection of the other occurs unconsciously. Now apply this to the example of a person you see at the health food store or the market or on TV or in the movies. Evaluating, labeling, and rejecting is constant and incessant.

Rejection Is A Façade Because It Is Projection

All rejection is first and foremost a rejection of self, not of other.

Let's say that you are in the market and you see a person who is hurrying and slips into the line right in front of you. You get in a huff because you feel like you, too, are in a rush, and how dare they not see your needs, or how dare they even try to go for their needs over yours?! You feel slighted.

Yet, what if a different reaction were possible?

One is.

Not everyone reacts with hurt or frustration, right?

Let's back up even more.

What if your aggression or annoyance with that other person is actually because you subconsciously still carry the feeling that your family never met your needs, or you feel currently that you are overlooked? Maybe you feel that there is a pattern in your life of people ignoring you.

Now, let's pretend you do not have that pattern. Let's pretend you grew up in a house as the only child, and you had attention showered upon you. The person stepping in front of you does not annoy you because you are feeling safe, and you trust you will get yours. All is well.

This is admittedly a polarized example, but it's how this all works.

I frequently say, "We are like walking movie projectors."

Picture your neck and instead of a head, there's a forty-five-millimeter film projector on top. That is how we are.

What if what you label and evaluate about the other has more to do with you than clearly seeing and perceiving them?

Because that is the case.

I differ from the majority of spiritual teachers in that I see about 10 percent of life events as random, and approximately another 10 percent are out of your control due to outside influences bigger than you.

Nonetheless, someone's seeming rejection of you may have triggered something within you, sure. But their rejection of you is more about them. Let's say you proffered love and they weren't ready to receive being loved due to having grown up in a very alcoholic or non-nurturing environment. Your offering of love throws them out of familiarity with what they've unconsciously labeled *love,* so your offering will be too radically different vibrationally for them to be able to receive. So, they say no.

None of that is about your body size, shape, hair color, eyes, profession . . . meaning, you're left with blaming yourself and finding something wrong with yourself when, in fact, it's not you, it's them and their inability to receive.

There is so much more territory of who we are and why we choose what we choose that is contained at the unconscious and subconscious level. Most leave this territory unexamined, so they remain at basically the same level their whole lives.

In fact, the stats are that at least 85 percent of the choices we make on a daily basis are made at a subconscious level. You are on auto pilot *way* more than you even realized!

Moving Beyond Duality Into Inclusiveness

In 2012, there began massive bursts of higher vibrations released from the center of the Universe. On NASA.com, you can see cosmic events and alignments, such as massive sun flares. Starting around this time and continuing into the present, I have worked more than ever before with people, such as scientists, bookkeepers, accountants, attorneys, marketing analysts, math teachers, and former senators. I have come to understand that, no matter their complaint or reason for seeking me, I was feeding Life Force into their systems to rebalance the focus of their consciousness so that they became less left-brain dominant and less focused on seriousness and problem solving.

They had presented with such accompanying physical symptoms as clogged sinuses, spacing out, or inability to focus. I use an energy medicine technique that is geared toward opening an access point that, once activated, helps the brain shift into whole-brain consciousness. This opening is also known in ancient yogic practices and other ancient spiritual disciplines. Opening the access point for these clients speeds up their spiritual awakening, as if they'd already been meditating for five years.

In addition to that technique, I use other processes and tools to help folks shift from left-brain dominance with its logic and analysis into a more balanced hemispheric usage with their innate and strong intuitive powers. An interesting indicator here is that when a sixth chakra—the *ajna* center between the eyebrows that corresponds to the pituitary gland—is closed down, it means we are ignoring our intuitive side.

Guess what another indicator of this imbalance is?

An over-emphasis on problems and seriousness.

We all have intuition innately wired into us.

What is implied when an entire culture leans more toward the serious issues and problem solving?

Overall, I find that I have been assisting people to better navigate the times we are in right now. I've given them a major leg up by opening them to a whole-brain consciousness, not just the right-brain/left-brain balance.

Folks who are used to being in the left brain and relying on linearity, logic, reason, and Newtonian physics—in which everything is concrete and sequential—are feeling like fish out of water. These higher vibrations have really been spacing people out.

Some people seem to have their capacities turned on successfully to make use of these vibrations without being rocked by them so much. They operate with a more advanced level of consciousness that is better equipped to not only field the higher vibrations but also make great use of them.

And yet these are the energetics that are the backdrop to life right now.

Have you been forgetting things more?

Have you seen time fly by, no matter your age?

Have you been more spacey?

Have you had a sense of someone before they texted or called and then, there they are via a text or a phone call?

This current opening asks us to enter a wholistic consciousness instead of a reductionist consciousness. We're being relatively commanded now into a brain, system, and life that is wholistic and connected to all life, instead of separate and on our own. This invitation is evident in all aspects of life, beyond the rewiring of our neurology, although the balancing of the hemispheres and the transcendence of duality into a wholistic consciousness is a large part of it.

This is happening not only in the West; it is global. Whatever adjustments needed are happening as appropriate to the individual and the culture and the language and the system they grew up within. This rewiring may make you feel destabilized. Another major source of destabilization I've seen going on for the masses is the crises that have split their world wide open. These crises are happening and have happened for a bigger reason. Remember—take the mountaintop perspective.

It is meant to make you feel destabilized so you come out of the ego-mind's preferences and are forced to go deeper and learn how to live in a flow with Trust and learn some yielding and surrender to something bigger than just what your mind can label, evaluate, analyze, judge, reason, calculate, and compute.

ACCEPTANCE PROVIDES AN OPENING

Both programs I use with my clients and students—specifically my signature program and my mastermind folks—are geared toward helping people more easily create or manifest what they want. People often shift out of doing a job that is dry and boring for them and into creating a business based on their passion.

I describe this work I do as *going beyond the Law of Attraction*. It ventures into understanding the flow of energy, and how that works for or against you within your manifesting, and how all life works together. You can dance with the kind of awareness I've presented here—awareness of the mind's activity and the possibility of detachment from the games the mind plays—and enter this whole other territory that allows you to engage with the Universe and the Universal Life Force Energy more actively, with more ability to direct it on your own behalf.

Labeling Slices; Acceptance Includes

Instead of simply allowing the rainbow to be the beautiful, magical, and uplifting aspect of life it is, we divide it up and say *red, orange, yellow, blah, blah, blah.* Yes, naming the parts is a kind of learning to communicate about life with each other. And yes, understanding how the spectrum of colors plays with refracting and reflecting surfaces, especially in drops of moisture after rain, is interesting.

Yet, to label something, we effectively remove it from the whole. We slice something out of its greater context immersed within and from the Creator, whoever or whatever the Source of the force is.

The helix of a single strand of DNA is a common symbol throughout cultures and throughout nature: the nautilus shell, flower petals, hurricanes. But the singular DNA strand does not communicate as effectively the Universe's innate understanding of what this thing is as much as the whole double helix of the DNA. That wholeness has a more robust ability to know the Universe and for the Universe to understand it than the individuation or reduction of something sliced from its whole to be labeled, judged, evaluated, and preferred or pushed away.

Acceptance Lowers The Drawbridge To More Energy

The studies mentioned earlier that have been done on meditation and spiritual practices show that the prefrontal cortex and the anterior cingulate both become more activated after twenty minutes of meditation. The prefrontal cortex does not complete its development until we are around the age of nineteen. That is why teens can seem so reactive. The reptilian part of their brain, the limbic system, the emotional part of our brain is developed by the midpoint of our teen years. And that is the self-management part of the brain. That is the executive control, the compassionate center, the empathic center. [3]

I mentioned earlier the studies that have been done on meditation and spiritual practices that show with the prefrontal cortex fully activated and even cultivated and developed further through the practice of meditation, the ability to empathically recognize facial expressions and what they mean is increased.

Compassion and empathy are inclusive. They help you reach out.

---

3 Coon, Dennis. *Introduction to Psychology: Gateways to Mind and Behavior with Concept Maps and Reviews*. Cengage Learning, 2006.

They do not push away with that force and aggression of the mind, right?

They help you reach out with acceptance. Reaching out is an invitation to something beyond the label, the judgment, the end of the story. Judgment is like a closed room with four walls and closed door. An open, circular room with an open door is analogous to compassion and empathy.

The anterior cingulate has been shown to act as a bridge into accessing the parts of the brain that are activated when someone feels compassion. When you live from the dominance of the ego-mind, it is as if you have been living in that closed room. With practices that cultivate higher, more evolved states of consciousness, you accept the invitation to more consciousness, to another possibility—not for you alone but also for those you interact with. These practices access higher states of consciousness. And this, the Universe can recognize and respond to.

The Universe is opening this gateway for us right now. It is not always comfortable because the most change is afoot right now, apparently more than has ever been afoot on Planet Earth for humanity. It may feel to you like a fever is peaking before it breaks; it may feel like the judgment, the divisiveness, the separation, and even the pushing force—the aggression, those attributes of the ego-mind that remain unchecked when someone is not working with self-management—are peaking in order to collapse into this other way.

Wholeness Invites The Flow Into You

We are talking about heart-centered living here.

What does it mean when someone says *being more heart centered?*

Let me present what is actually at work here.

All the way at the other end of the spectrum, I am going to bring in Jesus Christ. You may or may not follow him; I do not necessarily *follow,* but as a person who is trained in energy medicine, I have come to the understanding that Jesus Christ is the greatest healer ever to have walked this planet. Buddha was the most compassionate. Please don't misevaluate here. I am not saying Jesus was not compassionate—consider the huge teaching of forgiveness. What I am talking about is Christ-*consciousness* here, of that heart, of the ability to yield, of the ability to forgive. Sure, you already know that, you have heard that enough from the religious doctrine.

The more that you live in a yielding, surrendered space, the less that you live from a mind that divides, labels, evaluates, and pushes away. Then, the more access you gain to the Universe's magic because you are living from the wholeness. Remember, the wholeness is the aspect of the mind-body-spirit trinity that actually communicates with the Universe, and that the Universe searches for, hears, and understands. This increases your ability to join up, or yoke with, the Universe's Life Force, or chi, as well as your ability to effect the change you desire to manifest.

I've been teaching this since 1998. I have been flowing it since 1996. There is a preference the Universe has when it wants to join up with or yoke with some energy that is not judging, separating, or dividing. The Universe is a benevolent, loving force. We simply have to go through the initiation process of inviting it in.

What does that involve?

The ego-mind structures will collapse to some degree. Some unconscious and subconscious blocks will be cleared. It is the most sacred process a human being can go through.

It's like you're inviting the Universe to your own party—it has to be called in with a nice invitation.

Just like you when you chose that partner or when you chose that best friend of yours, you did not choose somebody who was busy rejecting you, did you?

No. You sought someone whose inviting energy you could feel. The Universe is no different.

When you label and judge, you shut the door and extend no invitation. When you accept and yield, you open the door, and your invitation is extended—and received!

The drawbridge is now open more than ever for you to enter your castle of this magical land in these Awakening Times. I do not think it a coincidence that Surrendering a clinging ego-mind, which has our most stubborn world views, feels like slipping through the eye of a needle. This Surrender is what I wrestle with while guiding someone, mentoring someone, through this opening—this is the wrestling match. And I have not yet tapped out.

CHAPTER THREE

Manifestation Is Easier When You Understand It's a Vertical Focus, Not Horizontal

SEPARATION DOES NOT YIELD EASY MANIFESTATION

Part of my work on the planet is to disrupt the normal way a conditioned mind robotically approaches life. When we disrupt the old patterns, other possibilities can weave themselves in. More of my work has become to tune in to these very possibilities and guide others to this magical meeting ground.

It's like when you're sitting in traffic on a clogged, six-lane highway. You're heading in the direction that has the three clogged lanes. You look over to the other side of the highway, and those three lanes are empty.

I'm over here in the spaciousness of those empty three lanes. That's what it's like where I've been communicating from—wide open space that comes from living in possibilities. The average person has been entrained to feeling scrunched, limited, and restricted—so, congratulations on even picking up this book and following your intuitive knowing. I'm glad you are here.

The Mind Contorts And Twists The Process

When you come out of being mind-dominant, it's like a towel you twist around your wet hair and wear on your head as you get out of the shower. If you want to dry the towel and put it in the sun, it won't dry very well twisted up in that shape. Expecting a bunched-up towel to dry is like someone whose mind is demanding: *Why hasn't what I want manifested by now?*

Now imagine that same towel, but it's completely open, lying flat in the sun. It's able to connect with and receive the sun's rays in a much more full and robust way. You want to create and manifest using your creative powers *and* the co-creative powers of the Universe. If the mind is involved with demanding *how* and *when,* that twists and contorts the process and delays the outcome.

Typically, if this is the case, what it also creates is a distorted form of what you were actually desiring. The Universe could have done a better job had you pulled back and allowed it to. You have myopic vision; the Universe's vision is omniscient. It has access to more possibilities as well.

Which vision is more logical to rely on?

Bigger And Better Than Ever Before

Learning how to live from the heart, in Surrender, will give you the power to enter the co-creative dance with the Universal Life Force. These two steps—surrendering and entering the dance—are the second up-leveling that is going on within our greatest evolutionary leap of humanity's spiritual awakening between 2012–2032.

The Universal Life Force composes and flows into and through the unlimited field of possibilities. They're one and the same.

The electromagnetic field of the earth, our mind-body-spirit systems, and the elements are always interconnected and exchanging information. Chi is composed of electricity and magnetism. The more chi you access and flow through your system, the more you access the field of unlimited possibilities.

Back The ______ Off!

To be able to approach the Universe and for it to work on your behalf, you must *back the ______ off!* This is the key step for generating the most robust support and power possible to create and manifest your most cherished dreams with pleasing outcomes that'll likely surprise and titillate you. It's the hardest, as well, based on what I've seen in my twenty-five years in the human potential field.

Backing off is stepping out of the ego-mind dominance. That means to a degree, you're going to need to come out of your identity, out of your storylines, out of the comfort of knowing your expected reactions.

Becoming new and spontaneous puts you more in the flow of Universal Life Force, or chi. Thus, you are constantly renewed. Also, you'll need to step more into the allowing of the new—allowing for creation by you and through you—rather than clamping down on needing to know *how* and *figure it out* before even initiating the change.

THE GOLDEN SHOWERHEAD (LOL)

Visualize the Stellar Gateway approximately two feet above your head. Once you've shifted and this faucet is turned ON, it pours down these higher, golden frequencies that create more possibilities, flushing your mind-body-spirit system via each individual chakra, lighting up you and your life. When you flip the switch or lever to ON, you make this overall shift. The *Golden Showerhead* (LOL) contains Support for you via Guidance and other means, and thus, this is what I see at the crown chakra, even starting at the Stellar Gateway—one of those newer, transpersonal chakras recently activated.

Your Team Of Support

It's funny—when I introduce my energy medicine students to the trainings and attunements, and they experience more of the Universal Life Force flow through their chakras, they begin to sense and see what they've been missing. Part of their initial training program is to work with my chakra attunement audio series, available at alisonjkay.com/chakra-healing-audio-series. Then I go through their systems when together live, clearing out their chakras. You won't be able to open and balance your chakras simply by watching a five-minute YouTube video.

The chakra system is an ancient science that still serves as a road map to enlightenment and thriving in mind, body, and spirit. Open each of your chakras, and thus the overall column, and allow this Golden Showerhead to pour its influx of supportive energies, from the newly activated, transpersonal chakras above your head. This is where these brilliant golden frequencies of our Awakening Times access us. They're there, wanting to infuse your system and life, so you can live from elevated possibilities.

For a review of the chakra system, which is a vast science, refer to my second book and my website for the chakra audio series. Here, I'll briefly say that a *chakra*—which means *wheel* from Sanskrit to English—turns the chi or Vital Life Force Energy throughout a region of the body, mind, and spirit. When blocked, it does not turn. This overall flow is meant to start from above the head, where your connection to your Higher Self and the Universe reside, all the way down to your feet on Planet Earth.

Unconscious and subconscious blocks may sit in a particular part of the body. This is dependent on the content of the block because of where the corresponding chakra, which covers this content, or part of life, is located. Each domain of life corresponds to one of the seven chakras of the 3-D chakra system, while the new *transpersonal* ones are just that—*beyond personal.*

If your unconscious block involves feeling unable to choose what you really want—for instance, because you feel burdened and obligated to provide for your family with a *safe* job and more reliable paycheck—that corresponds to the fifth chakra, located at the throat. This is the chakra covering courage, choice, and co-creation. Someone without a block at the fifth chakra would be more prone to taking a risk even with the demands of providing for a family. If your neck is tight, the thyroid is also likely to be imbalanced, either overactive or underactive. Each chakra corresponds to one of the major endocrine glands, so that the entire hormonal system is covered by one of the seven chakras. Ingenious design, right?

Without a process to clear the chakras, chi gets blocked throughout your system, resulting in little flow of this supportive Vital Life Force Energy. Since these Awakening Times have begun and the overall vibrational backdrop is higher, the goal is for all of us to raise our vibration and drop away the density.

What do I mean by density?

- Old karma
- Old fear-based traumas and beliefs
- Unconscious and subconscious blocks, like the ones I spoke of earlier

The gig for us now is to clear this density out of our systems—both personally and collectively. As we do so, chakras open, our vibrations rise, and we learn to live beyond the ego-mind. We activate all parts of our mind-body-spirit trinity system that now has the UPgraded vibration, due to its increase in flowing of this Vital Life Force Energy that's inherently higher.

This process of purification must occur before you can attain an increase in power capable of wielding the creative Life Force energies. And this you will do increasingly, the more you Surrender and Allow in this flow, as the ego-mind downshifts. Once you do so, you'll have more of this Universal Life Force not only flowing *to* your system, but *throughout* your system. The more energy you have at your disposal, the more flows to the external world, and out to your desired creations to give them the increased magnetism at the relevant chakra and the increased Life Force to help emanate your desired manifestations—again, at the relevant chakra.

You can get to a point where your consciousness, or the field of consciousness surrounding your body, becomes so aligned that it does not only the heavy lifting for you, but compounds your efforts, easing everything. And this is when and why I say, *Manifesting as if by Magic,* because it seems that way, compared to what we've become conditioned to believe is required to "make things happen."

Each chakra is a vortex, and the more open they are, the more energy they emanate onto the physical, horizontal plane of everyday existence. Couple these last two facts, and here's your recipe for your horizontal output, not input.

Yet to have this emanating power that puts out your requests for you, generating more momentum and more robustly moving energy toward your desired manifestation, it does seem like a certain amount of Alignment has to be in place before a person can be trusted with this increased power to co-create their desires out into physical matter. It is like you have to be pure enough of heart and intention, aligned with integrity, and able to surrender to the Universe's higher knowing and your Higher Self's higher knowing. And you must Surrender to that higher knowing without trying to force, control, twist, or contort the process. You also have to be aware of your little ego, who throws a temper tantrum when events or behaviors don't go as it wants.

The new transpersonal chakras above our heads are the *Causal Chakra, Soul Star,* and *Stellar Gateway.* These begin communication with stars, galaxies, and the cosmos. They really open us to all that is becoming possible.

I use the term *Golden Showerhead* because it seems that what we have been showered upon with are these golden frequencies from the Universe. I am seeing more gold now. It feels more golden. The Christ Consciousness is considered golden. Once you get through a certain level of purification, the Golden Showerhead turns. That allows more support in. I don't bother going into differentiation between *guides, archangels,* or whatever the team of support is around each of us. I just know it's there, so I show my students how to increasingly allow, access, and interpret this supportive team's intuitive messages and support. It really does grow; the support compounds the more you Allow it to and Surrender to it.

Turn It All The Way On!

From 2012 to 2019, golden frequencies rocked people into crises, which led to change. What wants to happen now is the creation of the New Golden Age. We are learning how to create the institutions, businesses, relationships, energy production systems, medical systems, food production, political systems, educational systems, and physical structures to live in that are all much more harmonious. They, too, are being purified so they, too, can be Aligned with integrity.

This level of purity must extend throughout a process; for instance, in the production of food—from growing the food, transporting it, packaging and preparing it, to the end point of eating the food. You can look at any aspect of life, and you can see the effects of this purification process and where some industries experience more symptoms of these effects than others. Some are slower—more resistant—to change.

I have been working with this Universal Life Force flow for at least twenty-five years. Increasingly, I am in awe at the recent assertion from this energy, one that demands: *Let me in!*

How to turn it all the way on?

First, by knowing this, and second, by inviting it in.

The Universal Life Force Wants To Help You

Prior to teaching AP Psychology, when I was teaching that Global Psychology course I created, a few of the texts I used were taken from His Holiness the 14th Dalai Lama's biannual summits, held with Western scientists every other year. At the time, I was also teaching English literature and there was a convergence between what I was teaching in my Global Psychology course with what we were reviewing for stories in lit class. I asked my lit students if human beings are inherently good or evil.

We developed our understanding from one of our texts from the Dalai Lama.[4] He said that the fact that we still exist is evidence that humans are inherently good. If we were inherently evil, the destructive forces would have taken over and we would be gone by now. He went on to state that over the millennia, we have learned how to let someone be the baker, someone the grain grower, someone the furniture maker, someone the blacksmith, and so on, so that we have all worked together to produce a village that works in harmony with each other to create life.

More recently, for a birthday present to myself and a gift to my students and subscribers, I went to the pre-Mayan ruins just outside of Mexico City, in Teotihuacan. When I asked our native guide about what he knew of the 2012 Galactic Alignment, he said that the old era, which ended in 2012, was the era of destruction. The new era coming in is one of construction, where we remember how to live in harmony again.

We have that spark of the Divine in each of us, no matter how you construe the Divine. That creative force to construct life resides inherently in the Universal Life Force, and this is the energy that flows through all of life. Even if you do not consciously admit it—that there is something bigger

4 HH the 14th Dalai Lama. *Visions of Compassion: Western Scientists and Tibetan Buddhists Examine Human Nature.* Richard Davidson and Anne Harrington, Eds. Oxford University Press, 2002.

than just us—you can still marvel at how your body itself breathes, the sun rises every day, and the oxygen we need is provided for all life to thrive on Planet Earth.

Understanding this for many in the West presents a learning curve right now, as does the understanding that we are inherently yoked with it. We can increase and reach out to yoke more with it. It is always there, loving and supporting us and helping keep us alive, even amid our own suffering, which typically is the result of our own choices from our ego-mind dominance and blocks.

What does a sunflower do?

It turns toward the sun, the light.

What about butterflies? Dragonflies?

How does Earth really sit up there in the Galaxy, aside from the scientific aspect of gravity?

How arrogant of us to think we could understand all of the Great Mystery!

What if we were to just let it love us and let ourselves love it back, and create from here?

Gravity exists so that our Earth maintains a rotation that allows us to exist. The moon in its beauty and glory gives us so many of the rhythms of the ocean and of all of life, including the menstrual flow. That is not random. Feel free to consider it random—but also feel free to consider that there is a higher divine order to this all.

It is a harmonious blueprint that you have on you *and* in you. Your system knows. It's just a different level of order than what the mind perceives as order, and what our science heretofore has entrained us to.

Many times, I have seen people's ego-minds, out of that fear of losing perceived control, choose to remain locked in a mind-dominant existence. This higher order is really like a warm blanket on a chilly evening. It simply exists all around you and asks you to use it, to wrap yourself in it.

Why would anyone resist that?

Because they can't receive that much love?

Perhaps.

ONCE UPRIGHT, THE FLOW IS HORIZONTAL

People tend to look to the horizontal world—to the world of people, things, and events—in front of them. This level is the physical third-dimensional world that was taught to us under Newtonian physics with gravity and concrete, sequential, predictable cause and effect. This is not where to start. This relates back to the mislabeling the mind does when people are learning how to co-create, align, and manifest more of what they desire on Planet Earth and in their lives.

Let's say you want to create a new business based on your passion. If you look at the world and you do not see enough opportunities to build your business—such as getting new clients, places to put up your business cards, or to speak at or give workshops—then your mind evaluates or labels the manifesting process.

You might conclude: *I am not meant to do this.*

But this is not a horizontal process, not at this stage of manifesting.

Now we know we are living under the Quantum physics energetic qualitative experience, in which there are quantum leaps and quirks, and there can be much more sudden and grandiose movement and change that doesn't seem linear. This is more congruent with the way energy behaves.

The Science Behind The Heart's Power

This is one of my favorite scientific studies to quote, and I refer to it in my first book: The folks conducting this study took EEGs and EKGs of peoples' hearts and brains and measured the electrical activity of each.

Which would you expect is stronger?

It's the heart, with *sixty times more* electrical activity than the brain, and that is with all the synapses firing with each and every thought! Estimates of thoughts per day are at 50,000–70,000. Now, add in the measure of magnetic activity, and the heart registers more than that—*five thousand times* the magnetic activity of the brain.[5]

If chi, or the Universal Life Force energy that comprises all matter, is electro-magnetic, then this implies clearly that the heart is *way* more powerful than the brain at organizing energy, and subsequently, matter. If that's the case, then by our choosing to cultivate more of the heart's qualities than the brain's, we are more capable of affecting our physical reality.

Have More Of What You Want

Check it out: Think of the visual of a lotus blossom's petals that you see around the symbols of each chakra.

You know how the lotus blossom looks when it opens, right?

The universal symbol for Buddhism is also the symbol for enlightenment, both of which are the open lotus. Each chakra has a different number of lotus petals. The crown has the most: a thousand.

---

5 HeartMath Institute. *Science of the Heart: Exploring the Role of the Heart in Human Performance.* HeartMath Institute, 2nd Edition, 2016.

Do you know that you can use each petal of the crown chakra to connect to a different planet or star?

I do not think it coincidence that, recently, several countries have renewed space exploration and new discoveries have been made regarding Mars, Jupiter, and the new planet, Eris. There is also increased interest in eclipses and viewing eclipses. Crop circles seem related here too. It is a cue from the Universe to pay attention, and many of us are responding.

The frequencies at the crown chakra are very spiritual compared to that of the solar plexus, which has more to do with empathic machinery to pick up on others' energies, metabolism, confidence, and power to manifest in the physical plane. It's a much more earth-based chakra, to help more with our experiences down on Earth.

Once we move up to the heart chakra, if approached from the root up, the heart chakra and all those above it are considered the spiritual chakras, increasingly. At the crown, there is such a serene sense of wholeness there.

It is like a hidden secret, veiled behind the red velvet curtain of the theater of the illusions of a blocked ego-mind. Again, remember this is the process of pulling back the veils, or the curtain that hides these secrets. Once you step through enough purification and initiations so that you are able to handle the curtain being pulled back, it can really become a qualitatively different existence, especially in these times, amid these Awakening frequencies. It becomes like living a charmed existence and in a castle of your own making, pulled down out of the sky and created here on Earth, in physical matter.

Sending Messages All The Time

Energy is our first language, not English, Chinese, Spanish, or French. Energy. You are constantly accessing and assessing energy. Typically, for the uninitiated masses, it happens at an unconscious level. But in fact, the third chakra accesses energy as you walk into the room or any environment. This solar plexus chakra has empathic equipment in it that assesses and picks up the energy of the people and the overall environment in the room.

It is the same with your heart chakra, but it is more about sending messages out, rather than taking messages in. With its pronounced electromagnetic powers, when this chakra is opened, and your showerhead is turned on so your flow is really there, your heart chakra then strongly emanates. This key chakra sings your aligned desires out onto the physical plane, where it meets with more Universal Life Force. It then is supporting you as things are becoming more easily naturally aligned. You begin to see just how much is going to be possible, where everything falls into place and you are *in the flow*.

When you approach doing something new that you don't want to be doing, and you have sub- or unconscious blocks around it, this communicates to the field of unlimited possibilities too. The field matches you, mirroring back to you that belief, without interpretation, just matching it.

I spend the majority of my time working here with people to clear these sub- and unconscious blocks. Next, I activate the relevant chakras to assist them with the necessary positive aspects of each chakra so they can more easily allow, go for, and align with what they desire. Their desires then emanate so consciousness can do much more on their behalf.

When those blocks are present, they communicate too. If we do not think we are worthy of a new relationship with the partner who's more brilliant than any we've ever had before, we're not going to find that person because we're going to be singing out vibrations that communicate this doubt. The appropriate response from the external world will come in a vibrational match.

This vibrational match will come in the form of a new partner who confirms those unconscious doubts, rather than the partner you really want, due to these unconscious doubts that you're not really worthy of the brilliant new partner. The Universe is always communicating with us. Learning to Allow it in—not just as support but Allowing in the mystery and the magic that is there, waiting all of the time—is another huge learning curve. It's a two-way flow of communication. It receives our energy, which is where our unconscious and subconscious blocks communicate, and matches our energy with its return communications, whether through a person or event.

This mystery cannot be controlled. It can only be approached with an open, pure heart. It's kind of like approaching a deer or a horse. But once you are there, it doesn't stop unless you stop being open. That is very much what I meant when I said I feel like Hansel and Gretel following the breadcrumbs of Guidance that the Universe and my Higher Self have given me to follow. I thus have been able to create this magical adventure that I have created as my life. I cannot imagine existing on Planet Earth without this two-way communication. It would be really dry of its aliveness and charm, and so boring, without it.

CHAPTER FOUR

The Feminine (Goddess) Needs Her Own Chapter

REBALANCING

While working out recently, I saw a commercial on CNN of men—only men—getting ready to go out. There was a series of about ten men going through the funny little mishaps primping themselves to get ready. One man was stuffing toilet paper down his underwear (socks use fewer resources!). Another man got a comb stuck in his hair and was unable to get it out of his locks—his hair just looked ridiculous. And on it went, running through other scenarios.

This reminded me of the gym that I used when I was living in Taiwan. I met a couple of different fellow ex-pats—including two Canadian men. They introduced to me a new term at that time, *metrosexual.* One of them had double silver earrings like George Michael's Wham! days.

He pulled it off because he had dark hair and eyes with olive skin, and was basically a stallion of a man who had a gentle presence and nicely chiseled body, and was on the cutting edge at that time, as a heterosexual male.

I remember him and his roommate when we were out one time, telling me about the primping that they do. I was thrilled to hear it was finally happening for the men too, that they would want to improve their appearances beyond the basics. I then became more aware of men taking care of themselves with waxing, t-zone care, beard care, more tightly tailored suits and pants, and prettying themselves to go out, taking the stigma out of it being only up to women to primp their appearances.

This is an example of what is coming into balance now, yet it is not about gender. It is bigger than that, although it does trickle down into some genderized shifts.

Since the start of doing this work full-time, I make accessible a document to every single new person as they step into working with me; the *Healing Response* document. It's a backbone of this work I do. Some say *healing crisis,* but I refer to the *healing response* regularly and frequently throughout the course of working with someone. In this document, they are given a description of what it feels like to go through the shifts, both small and large.

The healing crisis is synonymous with a fever needing to peak before it can break. A zit has to reach its full toxicity before you can successfully pop it and make it permanently disappear. Both are examples of the natural way our brilliant systems purge toxins. Unconscious and subconscious blocks are the same—our systems treat them as toxins—and both occur at the individual and collective level. We are in the midst of a collective fever peaking, as all the unconscious blocks that are out of balance are brought back into balance. It's in response to the overall higher vibrations pouring down onto our planet, orchestrating Humanity's Awakening.

So it is that our system is following nature's way. It is the natural course, and the primary principle of Taoism. It is nature's way to purge something before the overall block or imbalance can be brought back into balance. This frequently shows up as a fever peaking before it breaks—getting worse before getting better. I see many folks come to me having quit their process precisely at this point, not understanding how close they are.

The Patriarchy Is Showing Signs Of Wear And Tear

Each person has both the masculine and the feminine energy flows within them. Think of the yin/yang symbol. Each has particular traits and aspects to them; some show up more than others in each individual and culture, for a variety of reasons, including cultural conditioning. Within each side of the yin/yang, there is a smaller circle of the other contained within, so neither one is absolute. There are tools you can use appropriate for each flow, once you understand which flow is at work when and why you'd want to engage the counterbalancing flow.

For the last few thousand years, an element of the masculine energy that has been expressed is dominance. Power over something outside of ourselves stems from this urge for dominance. A core aspect to the patriarchy is this dominance.

This aspect of outward behavior—masculine energy flows—shows up within the structure of a corporation, for example, or hierarchy, where there is power-over, power-above, and suppression. An ensuing aspect to this is varying levels of subtle to overt degrees of force and aggression.

Think back to how the mind can feel like it is forcing or pushing when it has a certain type of attachment to the outcome. The part of the will that is attached to the ego-mind grows more forceful from this attachment to having what it wants, and to make it happen.

Force, aggression, and suppression, along with this power dynamic of power-over another, exist within a hierarchical setting, such as within non-Apple or non-Google corporations. This aspect of dominance is coming to the surface; this pattern is peaking.

The imbalanced aspects that still are out of alignment with higher vibrations of unity, collaboration, and cooperation cause the old masculine energy flow that became out of balance—dominance—to be brought back into balance. Competition is an outcome of dominance.

Ultimately, the feminine energy flows. Feminine energy, which leans more toward the internal, may be used as well as the masculine; and the two may be brought into overall balance. Peace, harmony, equality, love, and wisdom—all are of the feminine energy—must now harmonize with the old masculine for this new Golden Age moving forward.

In the yin/yang symbol, the black represents the feminine, the seeding of new potential, such as a baby. The moon corresponds to this inner rhythm and black color. The white color represents the masculine, the outward thrust, and the sun. The seeding has to occur before the outward expression. In following nature's way, a seed is hidden under the soil while we water and tend to it, until it is ready to thrust through the earth, emerging under the light of the sun with its fresh sprouts and eventual fruit or flowers.

Another aspect of this new Golden Age that Yogi Bhajan speaks about is how there will no longer be secrets. All is becoming transparent in this new Golden Age of higher vibrations that equal elevated consciousnesses. This, too, seems to be peaking.

Please continue to take that mountaintop or space shuttle perspective.

Bullying is another example of shifting times, as well as dictatorial regimes across our planet—they are coming up more to the surface, and we're talking about them more. That's precisely the old pattern giving way.

It is all wearing thin, is it not?

The way of power-over has been solidly anchored for a few thousand years. Where it has been able to dominate and maintain its power, it's accepted for the most part. But because of the more balanced and harmonious ways of the overall vibrational backdrop of the new golden era, the old and lower vibrations of fear/dominance/bullying are not able to anchor in that old, out-of-balance vibration.

It is peaking before it rebalances and as it rebalances. As we learn to evolve and live in a higher way, our vibrational backdrop actually catalyzes and supports this new balance, allowing the feminine to become increasingly anchored.

It Isn't About Rebellion As Much As It's About Rebalancing

Rebellion can include marches, protesting the patriarchal structure or control or the hierarchy of dominance of the 1–5 percent at the top and the corresponding suppression of the power of the masses of 95–99 percent underneath. In recent years, we've seen women's marches and the #MeToo movement.

Yet all of these actions in our more recent history are symptoms, again, of this fever peaking before it breaks into what it is desired to be created now. We must broaden our view of *rebellion* from solely these events on the physical, horizontal plane to the larger shifting patterns and rebalancing of power. Many say this is our *destiny* as a human population, with our evolution very much in our own hands now, yet catalyzed by something much grander.

In this current environment, it seems like a natural tendency to want to rebel against the power structure.

Taking that mountaintop, or now satellite, perspective, the rebellion could be part of you drawing your boundaries of the old abuse of power with your anger, right?

Anger helps fuel us to make changes, including saying no when someone has overstepped. Frustration is a milder aspect on the range of the anger spectrum, whereas resentment is a long-held, unexpressed form.

Revolution is not about only the pushing away or pushing back against because that force is still aggression. Instead, we need to complement that energy with a counter-balancing, higher vibration that absorbs those old lower vibrations of fear and greed, which lead to the desire for dominance.

Part of this involves wisdom. You gain some wisdom from increasing detachment to a specific outcome. You

Surrender to everything working out in a just way for the highest overall good, while—yes—still staying focused on your goal. Yet this is done from a lighter ego-mind and heart. You're in enough of a neutral-Observer mode in that mountaintop, now-satellite, perspective. But you're also able to be more opened in a way that then triggers and allows the receiving of a higher level of Guidance and Support. And this all leads to new outcomes.

Opening into Acceptance and Allowing for a higher version of these old, outdated dynamics now to be birthed is done very much in the heart chakra. Activating the heart chakra also brings in more of the feminine energy flow's aspects, many of which match the heart chakra's. The need for these aspects really seems to be showing up with this fever-breaking pitch as to what will actually evolve us into something new. Compassion, receptivity, connectedness, self-love, and self-nurturance all are examples of the heart chakra's and the feminine energy flow's inherent positive traits.

Expanding the heart chakra is how we bring in the new, beyond what we've known before, as we learn how to create from the Guidance and support of the Universe. The Universal Life Force flowing in and through us enables us to reach beyond the conditioned ego-mind for solutions.

Do you feel the resonance here with Einstein's rocking quote: "A new type of thinking is essential if mankind is to survive and move toward higher levels."[6]

I know that I am a part of the rebalancing as well. I am a weight trainer, just like in the Taiwan gym where it was almost all-male, where I was the only female weight trainer, and my westernized version of *the feminine* rocked their Easternized version of the feminine and masculine. Yet I also study subtle energy. My presenting the invisible via the higher vibrations of my cultivated energy is also a great part of this counterbalancing.

Over half of the rest of the non-Western, non-Northern world operates on the premise that the invisible is more important than the visible. Furthermore, demanding that we must see something before we *believe* is just old-school.

It is fear-based, power-suppressing dominance from a collective thought. We are afraid of allowing for the power of the invisible to be unleashed in the West again. Science and the Church were able to cultivate fear and tell us what to believe in. All of that is the old paradigm. It had its place and time, but it's on its way out.

---

6 "Atomic Education Urged by Einstein; Scientist in Plea for $200,000 to Promote New Type of Essential Thinking," May 25, 1946, 11.

Sticking even more ardently to science—even when the science is biased, encased within, and funded by that very same hierarchy bred by a now out-of-balance desire for dominance—is another aspect that is peaking. Those who want to keep the power and dominance call anything that isn't provable by scientific terms *quackery*. I've come to regard that as ignorant. Fear breeds ignorance.

On just a few of the massive number of interviews I've given, interviewers have used the term *woo-woo*. It hasn't happened on the majority of interviews. My response is to say that it's ignorant at this point to disregard at least half of what contributes to existence—the invisible. Fear and ignorance are intertwined in the Sanskrit term, *Avidya*. In the Buddhist canon it is commonly translated as "ignorance." During my yoga training in India, my Brahmin teacher of yoga philosophy said that this concept refers to ignorance about the nature of metaphysical reality.

Really, why is having to see something before you believe it such a very strong part of the Western patriarchal paradigm?

Who gains from being taught to distrust what is invisible?

In the East, people honor, respect, and have a sense of awe for the invisible, the magic and mystery in life. Sometimes this takes the form of superstitions because people view the invisible as more important than the visible.

In our ancient Western cultures, especially via the alchemists, it was the same. Paranoia from some of the seemingly nonsensical superstitions aside, they came up with mathematical and astronomical understandings that befuddle our basic questions around human existence to this day.

Are we really so much more *evolved* or *advanced* by dismissing the invisible?

No. Not anymore.

This is due in part to the over-arching foundation of rebalancing.

Universal Life Force permeates all life. It is unconditional love and support. It has our back all the time. It is there, asking to be employed for increased well-being and flourishing. In my day-to-day work with folks, this is what they're opening up to be and do, increasingly.

Universal Life Force doesn't want to be up in the sky; it doesn't want to be something we defer to in pleading prayers only when suffering. That kind of relationship would render us powerless, right? That's victim mentality, and that, too, is on its way out, as a central tenet of the old paradigm.

It is time now to learn to work with the sacred and bring it down into every aspect of our mundane lives, centering around our choice to co-create with it in both mundane and huge choices. That is what is coming into rebalance, too, at the grandest level.

Ignoring this energy would be like taking your mom's unconditional love for granted. We must appreciate and understand that there are invisible forces at play and learn how to balance them with the tangible. Then, we can practice working with both invisible and tangible, feminine and masculine energy flows, for harmony and balance, both in our own lives and collectively, in our post-modern, globalized culture.

This Is Way Beyond Gender

Here's some more mind-bending stuff. When I was living in Asia, I was intensively studying Kuan Yin, the Goddess of Mercy and Compassion. I had been studying her a couple of years prior to moving there because I wanted balance from the incredibly assertive masculine energetics I'd been engaged in both during my master's program in public administration and my job placement after graduation. I'd just felt so hard and tough.

Without even knowing I was going to end up in Taiwan, I had already been working with its iconic Goddess. Taiwan has statues of Kuan Yin everywhere. I would fill up my scooter with petrol and behind the gas station would be a seven-story-high statue of Kuan Yin.

When I first started working with her, the images I found of her were soft and feminine, perched on top of a lotus blossom—that symbol of enlightenment. Six years after returning from Asia, I began leading retreats and energy medicine trainings in Glastonbury, United Kingdom. Glastonbury figures prominently in the folklore of King Arthur and Merlin, the Celtic Goddess, the Goddesses of Avalon, and the Lady of the Lake. And for the first time in Europe in over a thousand years, a temple dedicated to the Goddess is now there too.

I have a statue of Kuan Yin in every room of my home, having shopped all over Asia for Kuan Yin statues. I scored a lovely quartz crystal statue in Thailand's Chang Mai's infamous night market, and another in India during my yoga teacher training, where many of the female goddesses are portrayed with anger. When I lived in Taiwan, I'd head up to the gigantic Taipei Jade Market at least one weekend a month. So, I have seen thousands of Kwan Yins. Each time, she had always been portrayed on the lotus blossom, in that soft, Chinese version of *feminine*. It was only when I got to Glastonbury that I first saw Kuan Yin on top of a dragon! She emanated both softness and fierce, raw power.

Two trips to Glastonbury later, I gave my first talk there about Kuan Yin and her dragon. Even though we are not talking about gender here, you can hear the implied gender roles about softness being the bill of goods sold to us as the way to be feminine. When you are being assertive or strong, that is typically considered a masculine trait. We've just barely come out of the time in which being female and strong and assertive gets us labeled *bitch*.

Expectations are placed on women in positions of power that aren't put on men:

- *Is she hot?*
- *Is she gaining weight?*
- *Is she compassionate?*
- *Is she kind?*

None of those expectations come into play with men; the authority is assumed.

I remember a colleague of mine who was a soft, kind, energy medicine practitioner. He told me that as a softer male he'd never get sex, but he'd get girls as friends. Somehow, softness has been pushed away from the traditional masculine gender lines but expected of the female gender. This is all coming back into balance, as we each embrace our feminine energy flow aspects with as much appreciation and glorification as we do the hard, masculine ones, and with the wisdom and understanding of when to use each.

These stereotypes of gender roles have helped keep locked in place this imbalance that has led to the dominance of the patriarchy, resulting in the imbalance of the masculine and feminine energy flows within each person. We *can* be soft men who engender gentleness and stability, and we *can* be assertive women who use power and force without manipulation. Each gender doesn't have to have a lockdown on the traits of their own gender's energy flows.

The stereotypes of each gender have served to keep this old paradigm at play for longer because folks haven't been in balance. They haven't had equal access to both of their sources of power, the invisible and visible. They haven't been able to work with the invisible and visible with both masculine and feminine energy flow traits. In the West, the favored model has been the strong male and the passive female. But you can see how that is no longer really aligned. Our men want to stop being the warriors; we women want to stop wearing pantsuits in order to reflect power.

Yet these stereotypes have implied preferences for certain qualities, and unconscious rejection of others. Much of this is cultural conditioning. I find when working with people that the words *yielding* and *Surrender* pose the toughest challenge to the ego-mind. The ego-mind has to surrender some of its dominance and perceived power to access this greater force that is closer to Source.

The words *yielding* and *Surrender* seem to imply weakness and softness. We unconsciously go to that assumption, especially within the Chinese culture, where women are taught to lower their voices as a way to be that softness and as a way to be submissive. Their job is to attract and lure. The culture creates the stereotypes there.

In the United States, we women are taught to rebel against this—that the female contriving softness or being submissive is one of the most strikingly wrong things you can do as an independent American woman.

There is resistance inherent to rebalancing. And yet, we are not talking about yielding to anything outside of you. We are talking about your own yielding within you, your own individual system, where your *you* yields to your Higher Self's Will.

Your ego-mind can be a spoiled brat. Its self-absorbed will is that it wants what it wants, when it wants it, how it wants it. We've been entrained to expect instant gratification and access with the almighty click. But learning to yield the ego-mind—that voice of self-absorption—to a Higher Will—your own Higher Self and thus soul, that eternal part of you who knows you are here to evolve, that part of you who yokes with the higher force of life, that creative force of life in the universe—this is Surrender, and there is nothing but Strength in this.

SOFTNESS FEELS BETTER, DOESN'T IT? (ACCEPTANCE)

I have marched in Washington as a feminist who doesn't proclaim herself as such—anymore. I have taken women's studies classes. I do not currently consider myself an active feminist in the way I was earlier in college and post-graduate studies' days. I am aware that I used to be attracted to this unbelievable machismo, hard-guy, bad-boy kind of a man. And I think most readers are familiar with that pattern, including male readers.

I look at who I have become as a woman and my preferences for my romantic counterpart. I came to understand this while I was living in Asia among Chinese men, because I found nothing hotter and sexier than a man who has managed down his ego and yet holds and centers in his power and can flow it, rather than use aggressive, forceful tactics to exert his power and dominance.

I dig women who know their power and do not have to passive-aggressively manipulate, so you feel as if you might step on shards of glass at any time when around them. I do not dig the ones who feel they have to put their viewpoint in your face in order to express it.

Women's distorted expressions of power indicate the need for the softening of the out-of-balance expressions of power. These distortions came from suppression. The need to soften applies to both males and females.

Softness does feel better. I prefer someone who feels soft to somebody who feels like barbed wire and thorny. You have to be careful around them because they have not done much work on themselves, so they trigger easily. And with little to no work within themselves, they are self-absorbed still, so being around them is all about them. And that does not feel good. And it is not soft. It is not welcoming or enveloping. As you can see, we are not talking about typical gender roles with terms like *softening* and *yielding*. The softening of the ego and the mind combined allows for the yielding to something bigger than just the small self.

Making It Happen Versus Allowing It

Taking action, making stuff happen, manifesting—these are considered masculine energy flows. If you think of stepping out, putting one foot in front of the other, you're taking a step that moves you horizontally. Jumping up and down would be moving you vertically. Taking a step is considered a horizontal, masculine energy flow.

The feminine energy flow is represented by the black color in the yin yang symbol, like the black of the night sky. The feminine energy flows are more about the internal processes like:

- Sitting in meditation
- Receiving
- Allowing
- Creating expansiveness or space
- Listening to your inner wisdom
- Receiving Guidance
- Seeding ideas
- Holding this seedling until it's ripe

Seeding ideas is like gestating a baby, holding it inside the womb, where it is shrouded in black, an internal growth process.

The heart chakra aspect is also part of the feminine energy flow, of an opened heart chakra being able to emanate what you desire. This emanation does some of the attraction *work* for you. Without an opened, emanating heart chakra, you're forcing, efforting, and taking more steps to *make* things happen, which are all masculine energy flows, and they are more ego-mind dominant. You'll also spend more energy this way.

Rather, an opened, receptive heart chakra emanating higher vibrations and your spirit's presence helps magnetize to you your aligned desires. Remember, the heart is five thousand times more powerful than the brain, magnetically.

You want to use this to your advantage, right?

This, too, is actively using the feminine energy flows in your life for your advantage.

From that emanation, your aligned desires are able to come to you, and from your opened receptivity, your feminine lines of receiving are opened, and you're in an ideal flow of energy to then magnetize to you what you desire.

The results appear while you have taken no steps. You have done nothing. The Universe simply picks up on your desire because your vibration is high enough and clear enough, and you're aligned, and you are broadcasting high vibrations through the natural electro-magnetic powers of the heart. Your desires are answered as if by magic.

You have within you a system that can do the heavy lifting for you instead of the more masculine approach of: *What is your goal? Now I have to figure out the how, make a concrete sequential five-step formula. Then I'll go after that plan.*

You force and push and assert your way through this, even when the doors are closing and you are hitting brick walls—you keep going, keep forcing, keep pushing because you are going to *make it happen.*

Feel the difference between these two?

Each Energy Has Its Place

The masculine energy flow is not *losing its power;* it's simply mislabeled as such.

The rebalancing of masculine and feminine energy is by no means about disrespecting the masculine, or about making the man bad, at all. I find much of this rebalancing going on within my male clients, who are needing to come out of that burdened *I Am the Hero* archetype of being the breadwinners, the hunters, and the warriors.

Learning these qualities of each energy flow with a neutral, nongenderized approach, with an awareness of each's role, and learning to use which when would most benefit whatever you're up to. It's more elegant, and ultimately requires less energy, than just plowing through life as a bull in a china shop, totally ego-mind dominant and living in resistance, while carrying around all this unconscious and subconscious density.

The masculine aspect comes into play after you have had the time to sit within your creative space. I do not mean simply to meditate. I mean you allow yourself to have a healthy second chakra and allow yourself to feel what you feel. If it is boredom within your cubicle or corporate job, then rather than dismiss it, not listen, or power through it anyway, honor this as the information it is. This is all the feminine energy flow. These energies have been undervalued and dismissed for too long in the West, leaving the masses in adrenal burnout and overwhelmed by keeping up with their obligations.

Listen to your internal GPS—meaning your feelings—not just your intuitive guidance. See what they are telling you. The dance now is between tuning in and listening, receiving information and Guidance, and engaging the masculine energy flow to take an inspired step outward.

New Tools For New Times

You can also see when you are avoiding change. It's a delay tactic by the ego-mind. The tactics used are typically under the guise of *needing to figure something out before you start*. The ego-mind is slowing down the rate of change. And when you do that, the ego-mind will say that it needs to have a plan, to figure out the how. That doesn't work anymore. Goals and plans. Strategies, wisdom, and targets, yes. But we're in much more alive and awakened times, so doing it more organically matches this vibrational backdrop. Interestingly, that also matches quantum physics and the masculine rebalancing with the feminine.

RAW POWER OF CREATION

The man I'm dating expressed how the power of women having the capacity to give birth was so phenomenal that he was rendered speechless. I found myself speechless as well, just watching him express his appreciation and awe. He was also saying that men unconsciously fear women because they have the power to birth children, and they have more power than men.

Women have certain wiring that helps us with that process of childbirth and momming. As I walk through the woods creating this chapter, I am menstruating and there is a full moon tomorrow night. So yes, feminine energy gives us cosmic cadence to our wiring, certainly.

I feel like we are also rising above the fear of that power and the subsequent suppression of that power. Here, I do not mean the masculine, but I do mean from the male.

That raw ability to hang within the blackness of the void and to create out of the darkness—the unknown, the womb—correlates to wildness. Meaning, the unpredictability of woman following her intuition and listening to her feelings has unsettled some men in the past. Listening to one's feelings is different from being at the mercy of one's emotions—emotional outbursts come from not listening to one's feelings and causes the system to get backed up.

When women were increasingly expressing feelings and emotions during the 1600s, it was labeled *hysteria* by Thomas Sydenham, an influential British physician.[7] It was the first mental disorder attributed to women, and only women. This was a catch-all for symptoms including, but by no means limited to: nervousness, emotional outbursts, and various urges of the sexual variety. The louder they expressed themselves, the more they got labeled *crazy* and were thrown into institutions to shut that right down, so it wouldn't catch fire.

I have noticed through my male clients and the other males in my life that they are also rebalancing. You can probably see that, too, if you think about yourself, whether you're a male or a female considering the men you are around. Some men are in total resistance, clinging even harder to the old masculine, which we are seeing at a collective level,

---

7 Tasca, Cecilia et al. "Women and Hysteria in the History of Mental Health." Oct 19, 2012. ncbi.nlm.nih.gov/pmc/articles/PMC3480686

politically, as previously mentioned. But that raw power of creation—well, it feels like men are gaining access to it as well. I'm not saying that men are going to be able to get pregnant, give birth, or start having periods. It seems like this raw power of creation is also part of what is coming into balance.

One of my favorite things to do is to unburden male clients from the programming that tells them they must be the breadwinner and the martyr. I have seen so many ripped up intestinal tracts from the pressure of competition and dominance men have and perceive they have, and from decisions men have made in business in which they've compromised their integrity. I have seen so many men feel trapped and unable to do what their heart really wants to do because they are meeting their perceived obligations of what it means to be a man and a provider. That's also coming into a different balance now too. It's a really exciting time, ripe with new possibilities!

Is this perhaps why the mystery schools of the Goddess throughout the centuries in Europe have been secret societies, and priestesses have remained somewhat on the down-low because this raw power has been feared?

Is this what was behind the witch trails, because that raw power to create was feared?

Just imagine the intuitive power that yields clear sight and having the ability to express it.

Who benefitted from suppressing that?

And what if now is no longer the time to be afraid, but to learn how to work with it, both males and females, so that we can actually be all that we are here to be now in a harmonious way?

What if now is the time for the expression of power to be not about dominance or suppression, but balance, unity, and harmony?

What if now is the time when we're each free to progress toward accessing and using the raw power of creation?

Perhaps now maybe more of us are ready to handle it again, in a balanced way this time.

Softness Is Power

What happens in your mind—what labels, evaluations, and judgments come up from the statement: *softness is power.*

Do you know that you access more power the softer you are?

It is one of the craziest things, especially for someone who grew up in America, conditioned by team sports and Hollywood because we expect the biggest things to be the most powerful.

But when working with the actual creative forces of the Universe, not from the mind, when learning how to step into being a co-creator now on Planet Earth of the 2012–2032 era of humanity's Spiritual Awakening, creation with the Universe and our Higher Selves does not resemble the sentiment that bigger is stronger.

When I am working with someone, they will have bigger shifts that are more tangible at the beginning, depending on how much work they have done before coming to me. Yet when we are working at a more refined level, those that seem to be quieter shifts are actually the most radical ones, with the most far-reaching effects.

The higher the vibration, the more subtle the shift is. The more invisible, the more subtle, then, the more power. It's another example of how the mind labels something the opposite of the Universe's or Soul's meaning. And I do mean the exact opposite.

Another neat little trick it seems like the Creator wanted to have us play here on Planet Earth. You have to love the Divine's comedic sense of irony. If not, well, that bitterness just won't help, as it'll keep you in victim mode, and you can't move or create anything from there.

Yielding Is Not Weakness; It Is Also Power

When you yield, you gain access to more power. Yielding is synonymous with surrendering. And it involves the surrender the ego-mind needs to do, where it thinks it knows everything and wants to control the way events unfold. This does not invite nor allow the Universal Life Force in, to yoke with you, and co-create with you. In fact, it keeps it out.

The heart chakra's aspects of yielding to this force greater than the ego-mind acts as a drawbridge rising, extending the invitation the Universe can recognize as: *Oh! You're ready. Okay. Here's some playful energy. Let's see what you do with it.*

But you have to be slowed down enough and become quiet enough to be able to attune to and perceive this occurring, so you can stay tracked with the cues and clues the Universe subtly gives.

The Mind Doesn't Create; The Creator Creates Through And With You

My audience and clients and folks who have been following me for years have known I say I feel like I've become a chess piece for the Divine. And I've felt like that for decades, increasingly. This occurs for my Mastermind clients and students too.

One of my master level students on our group call last night was asking me about using her Master level certification in Vibrational UPgrade™ Energy Medicine that includes Usui Reiki certification at a new space she could rent. As I was checking in with my intuition to respond to her, one thing that came through was that if my student took this space, she'd be close to a VA hospital. In this setting, my student would actually also—beyond the sessions for the individual clients—be grounding high vibrations in that location that really needs these more nurturing, unconditionally loving vibrations. Session after session, she would bring higher vibrations down into the space there for her PTSD Vet clients. And these higher vibrations would also help the VA hospital, increasingly.

Once you are more connected and allow in higher, lighter vibrations of the Source energy, you are more capable of grounding it down through your body as if you're a rod to run this circuit down onto the planet. When you step up, you are also being a vehicle for the Divine.

In doing so, in yogic terms, you are allowing yourself to yoke with your Higher Self's Will, which is within the fifth chakra. You allow yourself to yoke with the Divine will, more through your heart and crown chakras, and then you are truly in the definition of what yoga means: to yoke with your Higher Self and the Divine. You are truly in the definition of what being the co-creator means. You are truly living out what you are here to be and do in this time period.

You cannot get there from the mind. It does not give you the opening. Instead, it keeps closed that access to this vast and magical kingdom, as you can see by now. The mind is like a mousehole compared to the heart, which is like a huge castle with a beautiful drawbridge opening to you. The little mousehole is the old paradigm, where folks are living from unconscious programming that closes them off and limits their lives. That castle is this new life and new land that is magical and charmed with the Life Force coming in and down and through you, from our Source.

CHAPTER FIVE

Playfulness (Dragons and Unicorns and Fairies, Oh My!)

THE SCIENCE OF CONSCIOUSNESS CALIBRATION

Doing nothing often leads to
the very best of something.

~ Winnie the Pooh
in *Christopher Robin,* F. Boyce and S. Vaughan

In one way it is incredulous to me that I am presenting the science behind the value of joy and play. Yet, I know that it's acting as justification and further motivation for you to be less dominated by the thinking mind and its focus on seriousness, problem solving, tasks, and figuring things out. This way, with a more expanded, less closed-off mind, your consciousness is able to expand, and your heart is able to be more open and useful as the source of life it's meant to.

I get it; we're not fully there yet. Especially in productive, siesta-less USA.

The New Sciences: Measuring The Subtle

The Law of Magnetism that informs the much beloved, pop culture Law of Attraction body of work contains within it the Attractor Field Theory:

> The term Attractor is derived from the theory of non-linear dynamic and describes a subset of phased space (meaning a specific amount of system state) to which the dynamic system converges and which the dynamic system does not leave. This means that a certain value curve or subspace comes to and stays near the attractor *because of its inherent pull and potential.* (italics mine)
>
> ~ Consciousness Calibration Research Technique Blog

Remember the power of the magnetism of the heart, explored in earlier chapters?

Through the technique of neurophysiologic modeling it has been discovered that there are classes of brain neural networks that act as attractors as a whole . . . and are defined by feeling patterns. These patterns are actually dominated by fields of consciousness which reside beyond the body and are activated by choice. Thus, one's consciousness can be said to be like a needle in electrostatic fields of different dominance. These different fields have been calibrated on a scale from one to a thousand and are presented in Dr. David Hawkins's Map of Consciousness.

~ Consciousness Calibration
Research Technique Blog

Before we get to this brilliant map, it's key here to introduce the work of Dr. Rupert Sheldrake, who is one of the pioneering scientists I quoted extensively in my first book and interviewed on my radio show. He's actually the scientist who coined the terms *morphic resonance, morphogenic fields,* and *fields of mind.* He's been both a member of the Royal Society and among the top 100 Global Thought Leaders in 2013. He basically proved the science behind the field we work with in qi gong. He also describes the cultural conditioning that creates a *thought-field,* something I clear for clients when it's unconsciously or subconsciously blocking their progress.

I am extremely grateful to this man for his dedicated life's work connecting *Science and Spiritual Practices*—the name of his newest book. (Counterpoint, 2018) Sheldrake's work put scientific understanding behind what I already had been working with.

"Social groups are likewise organized by fields, as in schools of fish and flocks of birds. Human societies have memories that are transmitted through the culture of the groups. . . ." Sheldrake suggests that "the fields organizing the activity of the nervous system are likewise inherited through morphic resonance, conveying a collective, instinctive memory."[8]

I also see morphogenic fields around Facebook, Wall Street, and collective group endeavors, like environmental conservation.

Fear Is The Lowest; Joy Is The Highest

The calibration of consciousness itself became widely known from Dr. David Hawkins's Map of Consciousness as presented in his seminal work *Power vs. Force,* first published in 1985. Hawkins's Map of Consciousness is a numerical scale whereby one can measure the positive from negative, power from force, and truth from falsehood. Dr. Hawkins put forth that every word, every thought, and every intention creates what is called a morphogenetic field or *attractor field.*

These energy fields, Hawkins states, can be measured by a very simple process, an established science known as *kinesiology*. I know many of you are already familiar with muscle testing and kinesiology. Kinesiology is defined as a study of muscles and their movement especially as applied to physical conditioning, which Dr. George Goodheart first pioneered. This specialty he called *Applied Kinesiology*.

---

8 Sheldrake, Rupert. "Morphic Resonance and Morphic Fields: An Introduction." sheldrake.org/research/morphic-resonance/introduction

The study of kinesiology first gained scientific attention from Goodheart's finding that benign physical stimuli, such as beneficial vitamin and mineral supplements, would increase the strength of certain indicator muscles, whereas hostile stimuli would cause those muscles to suddenly weaken. Then in the late 1970s, Dr. John Diamond refined the specialty to *behavioral kinesiology* in which indicator muscles would strengthen or weaken in the presence of positive of negative physical, emotional, and intellectual stimuli.

Dr. Hawkins's research then took Dr. Diamond's technique several steps further by discovering that this kinesiologic response conveys a human's capacity to differentiate not only positive from negative stimuli but also anabolic from catabolic and, dramatically, truth from falsity.

Hawkins's Map of Consciousness reflects millions of calibrations of statements, thoughts, photos, art, music, influential world leaders in every discipline in almost every area of human endeavor. The research carried on for over twenty years to come up effectively with an anatomy of consciousness that reflects the entire human condition.

~ Stankov Universal Law Press blog[9]

---

9 Thompson, Carla M. "The Map of Consciousness: Hawkins' Scale." January 19, 2012. stankovuniversallaw.com/2012/01/the-map-of-consciousness-hawkins-scale

From Hawkins's *Power vs. Force*: "Man thinks he lives by virtue of the forces he can control, but in fact, he is governed by power from unrevealed sources, power over which he has no control. Because power is effortless, it goes unseen and unsuspected. Force is experienced through the senses; power can be recognized only through inner awareness."

Even more germane to our discussion he writes, "The only way to enhance one's power in the world is by increasing one's integrity, understanding, and capacity for compassion."[10]

On Hawkins's Map of Consciousness, 0 represents the lowest and 1000 represents the highest vibrations. So for example, shame tests at a calibration of 20, whereas Enlightenment calibrates in the range of 700–1000. In the Map of Consciousness, the lowest category is classified as "Life-threatening/life-diminishing calibrations" falling within the range of 0–199. States of consciousness include shame, guilt, apathy, and fear. The other category is classified as "Life-affirming /life-creating calibrations," falling in the range of 200–1000, with courage starting off as the first differentiating state of consciousness from the life-diminishing category on up to the life-affirming/life-creating category.

---

10 Hawkins, David. *Power vs. Force: The Hidden Determinants of Human Behavior*. Hay House, 1995.

Buddha and Christ both score at the top of the Hawkins's Map of Consciousness calibration of the most life-affirming states of consciousness. Reason is lower on the scale than love, joy, peace, and high creation, aka joyful creation.

Quantifying Your Moods May Be New To You, I Know

Driving in Asia as a Westerner is an experience in chaos. The likelihood ensues for the Westerner to label the lack of zoning and clear dividing lines between city and suburb as *chaotic*. But hang with me here, because you're going to get a sense of how there actually is order in the seeming chaos, both in driving in Asia and in your feeling life.

Let's translate the term *feeling life* into a state of consciousness. There is a science to this. It has been taught since Buddhism became its own science from the Naturalist Observation technique. The Yogic sages who came up with meditation Observed the states of mind. It was not necessarily calibrated with measurement and a numerical value, but it was understood that your suffering increases when in shame, guilt, grief, or attachment.

The lower states of consciousness that cause suffering are known in Sanskrit as *Dukka*, which means suffering. Suffering is a fundamental fact of life, caused by ignorance about our true nature, or the Higher Self. The root of the Sanskrit word *Bandha* translates into "bondage," and this term describes the typical ignorance humans get bound up, or locked up, by that causes them to lead a life governed by habitual, unconscious thoughts, words, choices, and deeds (*Avidya*) rather than authentic freedom, gained by gaining more wisdom, from clearing and purifying this unconsciousness (*Vidya*).

You have more freedom and liberation when you are in a state of joy or peace or compassion. You are closer to your true Self. Being and feeling are equal states of consciousness; notice the lack of mental state described here. That is because it has been managed, disciplined, and transcended so that it allows for these higher states of consciousness.

What would your life look like if you started to have these values?

You likely already do. And I thank you for being you!

But what would our society look like if these higher states of consciousness were valued, along with the understanding that egotism, fear, anger, and greed are all lower states, closer to ignorance?

What if you apply these understandings to the context of your power to manifest and create what you desire?

It is stronger the higher your state of consciousness.

Is that enough reason or logic to help you work with your own mind, with even more dedication?

Elevating your own consciousness works to your advantage so your life becomes easier and more aligned with what you desire.

CHOOSING JOY IS CHOOSING POWER

I am presenting to your mind with its preference for logic and reason the logic and the reason behind choosing joy. I want to let Winnie-the-Pooh (A. A. Milne) help me out in another moment here.

Did you ever stop to think and forget to start again?

What if we were to leave the science behind and enter into the Hundred Acre Wood with Christopher Robin and the land of magic?

When Negativity Seems To Be The Default

Okay, we're standing at the entrance to the Hundred Acre Wood and the land of magic, and our back is to society as it stands crumbling with the old paradigm, where negativity seems recently to be the default. Prior to stepping onto this path of enlightenment or awakening, or your own progress and soul's evolution, it does indeed seem like negativity is easier and more automatic.

But it does change. Know that. If it didn't, the yogic teachings and ensuing Buddhist canon wouldn't still be in existence and so actively sought after.

Each time you choose a higher state of consciousness over a lower one, you are creating a new neurological pathway. It's neuroplasticity, the brain's ability to change.

I know I said I would leave the science behind; but it's not quite so easy, huh?

It's so ingrained within our societal conditioning in the West to use science to validate anything. Yet Trusting in your own Higher Self's Observation of outcomes of each choice cultivates increased Awareness and Wisdom. You can make choices that lead to outcomes you desire more and move away from the choices that lead to struggle.

It is likely that you could conclude that negativity is more prevalent than positivity.

Especially in these times, right?

You could conclude that we are meant to be negative rather than positive because it seems like negativity is the default. But it is another one of those neat tricks from the Divine that remains hidden, until you start the inner self-exploration of working with your own states of consciousness.

We all agreed to do this at a soul level and signed up to experience life. Whether we actually progress and evolve is up to our own uniquely human gift of free will and the power of choice. Especially at these intense and simultaneously most auspicious times of humanity's spiritual awakening, it can seem like it is easier to access the negative and that everybody around you is also doing so. It may feel easier to be less patient, more greedy, and more self-absorbed as described earlier.

The Catalyst To Rebalancing

An ancient saying supports the concepts expressed through the yin-yang symbol: Going through struggle is the way we know what joy is.

We know joy, and access it, choose it, only by first knowing suffering. At a baser, less evolved level of functioning with your consciousness, yes, it does *seem* that way. It does seem like in order for the masses to choose something lighter, first they must experience darkness. The choice of higher states of consciousness is more likely made only when suffering in a state of darkness to such a degree that the suffering becomes poignant enough to force you to ask what else is possible.

This does have shades of the initiations that happen throughout this path as each person evolves by the raising of their own vibration and levels of consciousness into those higher states.

Yet, I have been asking since I can remember: *What if we did not need to suffer in order to grow?*

I have been asking for decades: *What if we could choose joy and grow and evolve proactively?*

Is it possible that this is eventually where we are moving?

Could it be that we do not need negativity or darkness or heaviness as the springboard causing us to then choose the opposite, more evolved states of consciousness?

Instead, perhaps that externally driven stimulus—of, say, a diagnosis, death of a loved one, a divorce, or financial crisis—is no longer needed. It could be replaced by intrinsic motivation. Crisis would not be needed to cause or catalyze someone to evolve or grow.

What else is possible?

Joy Commands More Energy

As you can see, joy has more power. Whereas states of consciousness—or *moods* as you may be more used to referring to them—such as fear, agitation, or self-absorption, are that forceful kind of consciousness I was describing, before even thinking about David Hawkins's work. Just the awareness of how the ego-mind feels to you, how you feel, when you allow yourself to be consumed by it, as it's pushing or asserting its way, is a lot of good information to Observe.

When the ego-mind is attached to something, and working in its mechanistic way: *I have to have that, figure out how, and I have to follow my plan,* does that feel expansive, free, and easy to you?

Can you perceive that as pushing and forcing?

And, are you relaxed?

More than likely, what you feel is force. It's the aggression of the ego-mind. It resonates with a dull, low thud.

Joy is a high vibration, as if hitting that sweet, resonant note when singing opera, a note so intense and pure it can break glass. When we are operating at a level of joy, we are in the heart, where more allowance and openness are allowed to grow. From here, we live in a higher state of vibration that allows us to move more energy. More possibilities are also welcomed as a result. We have more command over ourselves, or our self-management is empowered, and thus we are given more access to and command over the Universal Life Force.

Again, there is Divine irony in which the mind interprets joy as a by-product of something I do or buy or experience. The highest level on this path of spiritual awakening or enlightenment, however, is to choose joy *no matter what.* Joy is a choice. You could have that red sports car and still be miserable. You could have the love of your life and end up fighting.

Where is the source of Joy?

Turn within.

I provide you the science so when your mind is clinging to a state of worry or doubt or fear, you can tell yourself the rationale for stopping that behavior.

Accessing Joy helps you access more Universal Life Force. Nothing but good stuff comes from that, including your power to create more of what you desire and attract more support to create what you desire. When you are living in the lowest states of consciousness, you are more triggered by what bugs your ego-mind, whether about other people or traffic. When people start working with me, they lose these triggers quite quickly. After spending time with family, people working with me have consistently reported feeling less triggered.

Joy also accesses more power to *continue* having more joy, as the vibration becomes more entrained. Peace and stability are natural outcomes as well. You have more power over yourself and more power not to react to others. Then it compounds. Everyone's vibration gets upgraded.

When you choose Joy, power is restored to you—power to choose more joy and more of what you desire. You have more power to detach from what had been triggering you because the mind-body unconscious or subconscious connection to it has been cleared.

Joy leads to more power on many levels.

It's a very attractive idea, is it not?

It's not just an idea; it's what I'm up to day in and day out. I see the effects of joy in my clients' family lives and communities.

RESTORING MAGIC

People say nothing is impossible,
but I do nothing every day.

~ Winnie-the-Pooh
in *Christopher Robin,* F. Boyce and S. Vaughan

It's Meant To Be Easy If You Don't Mind

People who work with me and go on retreats with me, especially at the mastermind level, talk about how much fun it is. How much fun life is with me. I honestly feel like I am at a constant party and I have a permanent buzz and it is completely natural from all the work I have done.

I hear "Alison, I really appreciate where you have spoken about we're not meant to struggle."

Another common piece of feedback is, "It's your laugh that told me you're the mentor for me. I mean, you were talking about something so serious, and then you were able to erupt into that laugh!"

There is residue from the old paradigm that has conditioned us to be more prone to that which is heavy in life. The organized religions, for example, the depression era of our grandparents or great-grandparents, parents who have had it hard, all sorts of circumstances. Life has been presented as a struggle.

It is a lie and it is somebody else's mindset from another time, and you have the power to choose, to separate from that and create your own reality.

It is a lot more comfortable being with and around people who live from a space of the ease and joy—right?

When doing so, you have more access to the higher lighter vibrations, and you have more fun overall. Money loves to play with higher vibrations and fun rather than seriousness and fear and grasping; you love to play with that, if you want to attract a mate. Animals love to play with that. The Universe loves to play with that, and you will be brought all the different synchronicities via the animals and animal medicine communicating the messages to you that'll make your heart sing. Everything—when you let go of the investment in struggle—consistently, increasingly, becomes easier and more charmed as if you are living life like one big party.

You never grow up even when you are in an adult body, and you thus retain the magic that we are here to access.

It's Your Mission Now To Choose Joy Should You Choose To Accept It

Don't go getting serious on me and think: *That is not possible for me. I have obligations A, B, C.*

Oh, no. On some level you are making unconscious conclusions that say you have no choice but to respond to the obligation and even that it *is* an obligation. Do not buy the mind's seriousness and its conditioned habituation to struggle just because everyone else is. Because it is somebody else's lie perpetuated onto you that somewhere along the line you unknowingly bought in to.

What about returning that, getting a full refund now, so you can invest your money and Life Force elsewhere—into the ease paradigm?

The Unicorns, Dragons, And Fairies Play When You Play

I know this might sound a little bit *out there* for some of you, especially those of you who are like me—an intellectual, rational background, accustomed to using science to explain. But we said we were going to leave that behind. And we are going to jump off now.

It was presented to me that at one point on Planet Earth, eons ago, there was a golden age, and some say that was our Golden Age of Atlantis. There was no ego then. People were all operating on that high level of consciousness with unity, harmony, and joy. Dragons, unicorns, and fairies openly populated the Earth then. They were able to be with us because of our high vibrations. But once we entered the last ten thousand years of ego-based living at the fall of Atlantis, they had to go away because our vibrations did not allow them in. Our egos squeezed them out.

I recall reading in my thick, Western philosophy text in college a mention that Plato came out of the ocean and into Cairo, Egypt, talking about a great island nation that had just been flooded. I had a strong intuitive hit that he was talking about Atlantis. Later, I came across other authors' work mentioning the same thing. So, perhaps there is some historical data for Atlantis. Oral records became our written ones.

Switching back to dragons, unicorns, and fairies now, did you know that there is a dragon and sword on the seal of the city of London, and that the dragon was used to distinguish this coat of arms of London from the coat of arms of England?

England's country seal has a unicorn and lion as the symbols of the United Kingdom. They are in the full royal coat of arms of the United Kingdom, where the lion stands for England and the unicorn for Scotland. The unicorn symbolizes innocence. Unicorns are strongly associated with the feminine, and they traditionally appeared as a symbol of chastity, as well as the divine power that nurtures all living things. This is why it is often said that only a virgin can catch a unicorn. Purity is really what we're talking about here; purity is what unicorns respond to, apparently.

I listened to a talk by a UK Hay House author Tim Whild and his partner later on, Diana Cooper, during my first time in Glastonbury. They said the dragons and unicorns are back! That is, for those whose consciousness is high enough—read *purified* enough—to allow for this subtle connection in the subtle energies within other dimensions, frequently when in a meditative state. While we're here in our physical bodies on Planet Earth, the dragons and unicorns have become accessible again, ready to Serve and help us move into this next Golden Age.

I started to perceive the dragons as I started to invite them in more, and they responded by making themselves known more in these incredulous ways with the tinge of mysticism each and every time. I notice a certain scent when I encounter the mystical.

To clarify this, I was not seeing stuff about dragons show up more because of the same phenomenon in which you buy a red sports car and then you see red sports cars everywhere. It was not *my perception* projected onto 3D reality. Rather, it was their playfulness coming from the 5D or even higher dimensions into my 3D reality. There is a refined, yet noticeable difference between the two.

One night I was walking into the fitness center and on the benches right in front of the treadmill I was going to use, right where I was dropping my keys and sweat shirt, I saw this book. It's the only time I noticed a kids' book out here, away from the children's area at the back of the gym. I had been going there, nightly, for seven years. The lone book's title was *When a Dragon Comes to Live With You.*

Now that was interesting! I thought back to when I had heard Diana and Tim say when you open up to the dragons, they start to come in more to play with you.

Here is another observable fact: I have been using and teaching Buddha's most frequently taught meditation technique, the same technique for decades now. Yet when I used a visualization to connect with a unicorn from these authors, the amount of light that I perceived by the end of that meditative process was and is unparalleled! They say that the unicorns come in to help us more when we are aligned with being of Service. They come in to help us elevate our Service work on behalf of humanity.

Many, many dragons are back now, and they are at such a high vibration. They have different uses and purposes to help humanity and the planet evolve into this new Golden Age. You can invoke them to help you, but they cannot reach you unless you have that high state of consciousness, particularly pure joy.

They cannot get in, you cannot perceive them, if you are mired in struggle, fear, self-loathing, doubt, and worry. I wonder how much feeds into the mass consciousness's increasing interests in dragons and unicorns, with all the movies, toys, games, books, shirts, pool floats, and all the rest of the dragon and unicorn themes threading in. That's how something starts; at the collective consciousness level, before it hits mass consciousness.

We can feel like a hamster on an exercise wheel when we are in the lower state of existence. Which is why struggle, chaos, or crisis seem to be used especially around 2010 to 2016ish, with loads of personal crises used to catalyze people out of their lowest states of mind to seek a solution. In the seeking of that solution, many ended up seeing a crack in the veil. And their veils of reality and what had created that reality were forever changed. They can't go back—none of us can. This is so that something greater than just their ego-mind and personality and what they know, which is how they got to the crisis, could find its way in.

Once you have done substantial amounts of clearing and raised your vibration and UPgraded your overall vibration of your mind-body-spirit system, you do get to a point at which you naturally exist in a state of joy. You must continue to choose it; you do not just stay blissed out. But it's way easier as you're more prone due to the new biochemical and physiological set points. The new neurological pathways that support this newer behavior to grow the new state of joy, rather than perpetuate that old state.

In your new state of joy, the dragons and unicorns can stay with you, but this is not about just the dragons and the unicorns. It is about all the playful magic that we seemed to let go of once we become serious students for our college entry, and then serious adults in our serious careers, and a serious civilization based on reason, organized religions, and science.

If you look up the Cottingley Fairies referred to in the movie *Fairytale: A True Story,* you could explore for yourself what the impacts of actually being able to catch fairies on film poses, as did two girls—Frances and Elsie Cottingley—in the English countryside.

There was controversy around the authenticity, as one might expect, of these photos. The connotations of what this might mean, should fairies actually have been caught on film would be and was paradigm shattering—even in such spiritually friendly times as the late-nineteenth, early-twentieth century with the Spiritualist movement that Sir Arthur Conan Doyle was so much a part of in England.

Decades later, the girls admitted that four of five photographs were staged. However, Frances maintained the fifth photograph was real, and that she had, in fact, seen fairies as a girl.

As it is with all of this path, you can look to as much evidence as possible, and then ultimately defer to your own inner Knowing. Yet, from my own experience—and much as I'm writing about here in this book—these are playful forces, within the elements in particular. And the more we believe in them, the more invited they feel to come out and play.

The disbelief and the requirement of proof continues to act as that veil and keeps one stuck in the ego-mind and head and figuring stuff out, which these playful forces simply don't like, nor do they resonate with. These, again, are heart-based activities and beings, so the head requiring solid proof basically pushes access to them coming out to play, away.

However, an open heart who believes in there being more magic to this existence than what can be proven, or even seen with the physical eyes, is *the* invitation they require. Ah—the divine comedy of the Great Mystery.

Yet it just seems like it's taunting and tempting us now more than ever to come out and play!

You get more love the more joyous you are. And the dragons, unicorns, dragonflies, butterflies, the rainbows, the leprechauns, the fairies, the gnomes, Winnie-the-Pooh, are all waiting for you in your adult years. Yes, it's true. I live it and turn on others every day to doing the same, which they then do.

What if There's Nothing Wrong, what else becomes possible? A Conspiracy for Our Bliss?

Seems like we're finding out.

You wanna come out and play?

Conclusion

I wonder if perhaps you have the same sense I've lived my life with—as that detective sussing out the Universe's clues?

If you add one plus one and sometimes get two, sometimes get three, and even other times get five, this is how it happens with the Great Mystery.

I wonder if this book is part of that for you?

There is this element of magic within which our ancestors lived. Their technology in some ways was more advanced. It seems like some of the most recent discoveries at these ancient sites indicate this cleaner technology that was, in fact, more advanced.

For example, how did those three-ton rocks get moved in Stonehenge and become the new rocks there?

What kind of technology was used to build Stonehenge, the pyramids in Giza, the pre-Mayan and Mayan ancient pyramids and sites that cause us awe?

How did the ancients do this?

Really, out of everything I have seen, now is the time. There is so much more support available to step into living the version of your life that you had fleeting but memorable insights into as a kid, and in your dreams that stay with you once awake, and in your most inspirational moments when you have been at the top of a great mountain or watching a beautiful sunset on the beach.

It's not supposed to be only on special occasions that you experience this. I experience life like this daily. There's an increase in both traveling to sacred sites and power places, and an increase in people's desiring more of a connection to the etheric and less of the connection to their thinking mind. This further indicates that we are indeed in Humanity's Spiritual Awakening times. It seems like the Universe is showing us this, wooing us with clues, as if pointing the way.

Synchronistically, just now as I type this, a large red-headed pileated woodpecker has been calling out to me from a tree right outside my window here.

Now that I've acknowledged it, guess what?

It stopped crying out! Wow. I'm not kidding; there was so much noise coming from the trees outside that I had to go look. And now, it's totally still and silent.

Google "symbolism; woodpecker."

I would be grateful for you to allow me to help. I am grateful for who you are on this planet, for reading all the way through this book. You are special. You are meant to be here now. You are blessed.

And so it is.

Next Steps

Anything, *anything* that's going to lead you to inspiration and take you out of where you have become seemingly stuck or stagnant, please—understand that stagnancy is there because we are meant to constantly be evolving. I would love it if you wanted to hear and learn more.

I have a robust body of work. There are plentiful interviews I have given throughout the years to such outlets as NBC and with Dr. and Reverend Michael Beckwith who appeared in the movie *The Secret* and on *Oprah*. I've worked with Dr. Bruce Lipton the Founder of the Epigenetics Theory, and with physicist Amri Goswami, both of whom appear in the movie *What the Bleep Do We Know?*. I've worked with Krishna Das, with David Wolfe, the fellow longevity superfoods nutritional pioneer, and many more, all of which is available to listen to on the media and press page on my website: alisonjkay.com/media-and-press.

And if you are feeling like more than a visit, or that you, in fact, want to get actively started on clearing yourself, then join the thousands of folks who have used my Chakra Attunement Audio Series. You can see many of them raving about how the series and its clearing and activations within the MP3s have riveted them and improved their lives more than their expectations, and how they continue to use it for activations years after purchasing it.

There are sample clearings and activations for each chakra, next to each one's list of mental, emotional, spiritual, physical, and traumatic blocks, so you can also self-assess. But the biggest bang for your buck is purchasing the entire series and starting to listen today: alisonjkay.com/chakra-healing-audio-series.

If you want to really fast-track yourself, then this next step is for you: If what I have spoken about in this book has resonated deeply within you, if you want to lower the drawbridge to access it all, if you want to create your castle of living in a magical land of your creation, you can now step out onto the playing fields and advance your progress in quantum leaps.

Book an Open the Drawbridge call with my team so we can start moving you forward, helping you live that robustly, magical charmed life that you are here to live. It would be my honor to speak with you. alisonjkay.com/work-with-me

Please stop giving in to your mind and the thoughts that cause you to hesitate your movement forward. You will be doing your part in this greater Universe by choosing the lighter choices.

When I say the lighter choices, I mean choices that light you up because as you walk around lit up, you light others. And we are all part of a greater collective. We are all connected. That is why I do the work I do. This is my political action.

As we light up and raise our vibration and open our hearts, we affect the Collective; we help other people without even having the intention to help others. The old calibration used to be that one person awakened and affected 10,000 people helping them to awaken. Not even by saying anything outwardly, just by their vibration. Now with the vibrational backdrop of being immersed in Humanity's Spiritual Awakening, one person with an awakened heart now helps 100,000 people awaken.

We have already shifted the mass consciousness; we have already crossed the threshold. Please do not give in to the darkness. Please do not give in to the complaining mind. Always reach for what makes you feel lighter. The other, that which does not allow you to feel lighter, is simply not real, so stop making it so. We grow *up*, plants grow *up;* nothing grows down. We are meant to expand, not contract. Please do whatever it takes. Get yourself and keep yourself connected to this expansive field of grace that breeds constructive living as you unplug from the diminishing circuits of destruction.

About the Author

Dr. Alison J. Kay has worked as a Master Mind-Body Energy Medicine pioneer for more than twenty years. A world traveler who lived and worked at International Schools in Asia for ten years, she currently facilitates energy healings through her various programs and offerings for clients worldwide.

During her experience in Asia, Alison completed her PhD as a Holistic Life Coach. She continued fiercely studying Buddhism and Buddhist meditation, while also learning and eventually teaching qi gong and traditional Chinese and other Asian holistic treatments. Prior to returning home, Dr. Alison went to India and became a Yoga Alliance certified yoga and meditation teacher.

She created the Vibrational UPgrade™ System after spending years in Asia studying subtle energy. Her system presents the intersection of the mind, body, and spirit applied to cultivating vitality, health, longevity, and overall well-being. During her speaking engagements, she consistently awes her audiences with the completeness and accuracy from both her words and Presence, from which the audience further awakens.

Dr. Alison's business has won many awards, including the local County Advisory Board's "Creating Pinellas," an unexpected prize, declaring Dr. Alison's business as a contribution to Pinellas county, the second-largest county in Florida, and its residents. The successes Dr. Alison's clients have experienced in working with her have earned her the title of Number One Energy Healer on Thumbtack's app for two consecutive years. Recognition for Dr. Alison's first book, *What If There's Nothing Wrong?*, includes being awarded one of the top twelve Most Spirited Female-Authored Books. Her second book, *Vibrational UPgrade™ A Conspiracy for Your Bliss: Easing Humanity's Evolutionary Transition* became an international best-seller.

Dr. Alison currently resides in Florida, teaching local workshops and classes in mind-body fitness, yoga, and meditation. She holds a specialized certification in personal training for fitness and longevity nutrition, and she is a behavioral change specialist.

Made in the
USA
Monee, IL

15352164R00095